Growing From Within

A Study in Self-Actualization

Growing From Within

A Study in Self-Actualization

N.E. Bhagyavathy

PRESTIGE

PRESTIGE

Published by
Prestige Books
3/28, East Patel Nagar, New Delhi 110 008
in association with
Indian Society for Commonwealth Studies
New Delhi

ISBN : 81-85218-30-7

Jacket design by
Three-A Corporation
New Delhi 110 002

Phototypesetting by
Laser Impressions
New Delhi 110 028
Ph. 537296, 537756

Printed at
Mehra Offset Press
New Delhi 110 002

CONTENTS

List of Tables

What you cannot as you would achieve,
You must perforce accomplish as you may.

Shakespeare, *Titus Andronicus*
(II, i, 105-106)

The Humanistic Approach

As Murray (1948) rightly pointed out, "the main body o psychology started its career by putting the wrong foo forward and it has been out of step with the march of science much of the time." It is unfortunate that psychology, insteac of beginning with the studies of the whole person adjusting to a natural environment, began with studies of a segmen of a person responding to a physical stimulus in an artificial laboratory environment.

The chief consequence of this false start has been the undue influence of science in general, and physicalist method in particular, upon psychologists. (Heisenberg, 1958) After emerging as an independent discipline during the middle of the 19th century, psychology has been going through an adolescence. As an adolescent, psychology had valued little what its parents, the humanities and philosophy, could give, while it has modelled itself on the glamorous outsider, physics. (Bugental, 1963) As a result, psychologists tended to view the humanities as merely descriptive, historical, or ideographic, thereby relating them to a lower rank in the hierarchy of knowledge.

During the first half of the present century, psychology, in attempting to make the physicalist method its own, has restricted the grasp of its subject over and over again in order to adapt itself to the standards of physical sciences. Psychologists, in their efforts to be rigorously scientific, have often tended to concern themselves with relatively peripheral and fragmentary phenomena that happen to be amenable to objective and controlled scientific investigation. The result has been to focus scientific attention on those aspects of behaviour which can be explained in terms of conditioned responses. Thus, psychology had been projected as a science based entirely on the quantitative evidence and determinism.

Modern determinists of psychology took their lead from the 17th century English philosopher, John Locke, who concluded that the human mind at birth is a "tabula rasa" or blank tablet, on which learning and experience write their script, thereby giving the mind its content and structure. They view man as an object acted upon from outside by various forces, or driven from within by other forces like thirst, hunger and sexual appetite.

This view of man as an essentially passive, reactive organism is exemplified by the behaviorist and psychoanalyst schools of psychology. Behaviorism originated in a sensible reaction against anthropomorphizing animal psychology. But the pendulum has swung too far, with the result that it has rodentomorphized human psychology, studying the person as if he were just a complicated white rat. In its most extreme form, behaviorism has regarded the individual as a sort of mental robot. To put it in a nutshell, behaviorists see man in the image of a machine studying him as an object.

The psychoanalytic image of man is that of an instinct driven creature who secondarily rises to become an adapted member of society. Brought up under the influence of the strongly deterministic and positivistic philosophy of the 19th century science, Freud regarded the human organism as a complex energy system consuming and expanding energy. According to him, instincts are the sole energy sources for man's behaviour which is nearly always the product of an interaction among the three systems of the id, the age and the super ego. Discovering the process of repression of conflicts and guilts into the unconscious, Freud theorized that all human conflicts resulted from the clashes of the individual's wishes with the reality's obstacles and society's demands. He saw the working of conscience essentially in the guilt feeling that society, through the parents, instils into the mind of the child set on wish-fulfilment. Thus, both "the mindless technology of behaviorism" and "the poetic mythology of psychoanalysis" present us with a highly one sided view of man. Thus, the behaviorism describes man as a creature of habits and psychoanalysis makes him a blind victim of his past.

In recent years, however, a crescendo of voices has stressed the need for reexamining the basic assumptions of behaviorism and psychoanalysis. No doubt, both have made a significant contribution to the study of man. Behaviorism developed a rigorous objective methodology, and psychoanalysis suggested a global theory of human dynamics. Nevertheless, neither is completely satisfactory. For, behaviorism lightly dismisses mental activities as behaviour conditioned by verbal community, or ignores such activities as unknowable in any precise way. Orthodox psychoanalysis fails to do justice to normal personality. The exaggerated role of the id with its blind, self-centered obsession with bodily pleasure seems inappropriate to explain the detached outer-directed striving of a normal healthy individual.

The failure of behaviorism and psychoanalysis to produce a truly comprehensive and adequate theory of human personality from our existing orientations has brought into being a new movement, humanistic psychology, which is often referred to as a "Third Force." The writings of James (1942), Fromm (1947), Allport (1950), Cantril (1950), May (1958), Maslow (1959), Rogers (1961) and of many others have paved the way for the emergence of humanistic psychology. The humanistic approach to the study of personality rejects both the psychoanalytic and the behavioristic conceptions of human nature as too mechanistic, portraying people as passive creatures helplessly buffeted about by internal instincts or external stimuli. It is less concerned with motivational constructs as explanations of behaviour than with the individual's perceptions of himself, his immediate experience and his personal view of the world.

The humanistic approach includes a number of theories which, though different in some respects, share a common emphasis on man's potential for growth, self-direction and freedom of choice. The humanistic theories are fundamentally concerned with the "self" and the individual's subjective experiences. While acknowledging that human behaviour is influenced by the individual's culture, this new school of psychological thought empathizes that a personal factor also operates, and that there is a subjective side of culture. It looks upon man as a purposive and striving creature continuously engaged in the meaningful activities of choosing, judging and organizing. From this,it is clear that psychology has turned again to its ancestors—humanities and philosophy—from whom it has taken new strength to meet the challenges of our times.

The term, humanistic psychology, may be misleading since "humanism" has usually been associated with the Renaissance Movement of the 16th century England. The term also conjures up memories of ancient classics. But the psychologists use the term to merely imply an attitude towards psychology that stresses the adjective rather than the noun in the "human animal." As Krutch (1959) points out, a "humanist is anyone who rejects the attempt to describe or account for man wholly on the basis of physics, chemistry and animal behaviour. He is anyone who believes that will, reason, and purpose are real and significant; that value and justice are aspects of a reality called good and evil and rest upon some foundation other than custom; that consciousness is so far from being a mere epi-phenomenon; that it is the most tremendous of actualities; that the unmeasurable may be significant or, to sum it all up, that those human realities which sometimes seem to exist only in the human mind are the perceptions, rather than merely the creations of that mind." To put it in Shakespearean terminology, a humanist is anyone who says that there are more things in heaven and earth than are dreamt of in the positive philosophy.

Humanistic psychology aims at introducing a new "orientation" to psychology rather than a "new" psychology. Its role has been defined by Sutich (1962) as follows:

"Humanistic psychology is primarily an orientation towards the whole of psychology rather than a distinct area or school. It stands for respect for the worth of a persons, respect for differences of approach, open-mindedness as to acceptable methods, and interest in exploration of new aspects of human behaviour. As a 'third force' in contemporary psychology, it is concerned with topics having little place in existing theories and systems e.g. love, creativity, self, growth, organism, basic need-gratification, self-actualization, higher values, being, becoming, spontaneity, play, humour, affection, naturalness, warmth, ego-transcendence, objectivity, autonomy, responsibility, meaning, fair-play, transcendental experience, peak-experience, courage and related concepts."

Humanistic psychology acclaims that man is more than the sum total of our empirical observations. While recognizing man's reactiveness, the humanistic psychologist regards this as less distinctive of the human experience and tends to look to those ways in which human beings distinguish themselves from objects, from lower animals, and from one another in conceptual thinking, vicarious experiencing, imagination, communication, invention and discovery, mystical concern, inquiry and artistic creation. He discards the notion "nothing but" and tirelessly asks "what more may be potential?" Thus, man is seen to be at an early stage in the evolution of his own possibilities.

Naturally, the humanistic approach to the study of personality has a sharp contrast to the behavioristic approach. Behaviorist psychology has dwelt more upon man's frailties than it has upon his strengths. It has thoroughly explored his sins while neglecting his virtues. It has seen life in terms of man making desperate attempts to avoid pain rather than in his taking active steps to gain pleasure and happiness. It has dealt with man's misery, conflict, shame and hostility, being little concerned itself with man's gaiety, exuberance, love and well-being. In short, behavioristic psychology has voluntarily restricted itself to only half of its rightful jurisdiction—the darker and the meaner.

Humanistic psychology has undertaken to supply the other half of the picture—the brighter and the better half—so that it may give a portrait of the whole man.

The humanistic orientation differs from the behavioristic in a number of ways. The humanistic psychologist disavows as inadequate and even misleading descriptions of human functioning and experience based wholly or in large part on sub-human species. He insists that meaning is more important then method in choosing problems for study, in designing and executing their result. He gives primary importance to man's subjective experience and secondary importance to his actions. Further, he is concerned with the individual, the exceptional, and the unpredicted rather than seeking only to study the regular, the universal and the conforming. (Wilson, 1967) He seeks that which may expand or enrich man's experience and rejects the paralyzing perspective of "nothing-but-thinking." In brief, whereas behavioristic psychology has taken as its goal this attainment of the ability to describe, to predict and to control objects—animal, human and subhuman, humanistic psychology seeks to describe man and their experience that they will be better able to predict and control their own experience. (Bugental, 1966)

Also, humanistic psychology contrasts itself sharply with mechanomorphic psychology. Mechanomorphic psychology assumes that it must first find the basic units and laws of human behaviour and with these build an embracing abstract structure from which understanding of any particular event may be derived. Thus, being impatient with inquiries into naturalistic human experiences, the mechanomorph prefers the reductive and abstract. In contrast, the humanistic psychologist, subjective-oriented as he is, accepts the relentless challenge of a subject matter. He knows that he will never be able to encompass it fully and he finds his reward in his very engagement with a meaningful portion of that immensity. The mechanomorphic psychology is typically concerned with demonstrating that any new human behaviour or experience is really nothing but a variant on some already known and simpler phenomenon. The humanistic psychologist, on the other hand, is typically concerned not only to describe the existing way of the human experience but also to ask how it might be extended, enriched, or made more meaningful.

The crux of the issues between the humanistically inclined and other psychologists is methodological. The former tend to be problem-oriented and the latter are technique-oriented. Many of the technique-oriented investigators shun personality and other complex areas because they cannot be dealt with easily and neatly by the favoured means. Humanistic psychology seeks to develop methods for enlarging and enriching human experience. Typical of this attitude are studies of influence which act to limit our experience, (Harman, 1967) studies of the ways of breaking free of these influences, (Wilson, 1967) and of further potentialities. (Maslow, 1967) Besides, humanistic psychology is much involved with work in helping human beings to grow and evolve more fully in realization of their potential. Thus, work in psychotherapy (Haigh, 1967; Whitaker and Warkentin, 1967) and in sensitivity training (Rogers, 1967) is very centrally within the humanistic purview. It is also inevitably involved with the social ambience of which it is a part. It endeavours to study and seek solutions to the problems of war, death and peace (Lifton, 1964; Levine, 1963) which all human beings experience.

The primary aim of all the humanistic psychologists is to help the individual become the best possible version of himself as a human being, as defined by his own values, aspirations and limitations. They are primarily concerned with man's potential, his uniqueness and dignity as well as with methods of study, based on their affection for and joy in human nature. They are also concerned with man's higher needs—justice, order and love—and his pursuit of intrinsic and ultimate values of perfection, goodness, beauty and truth.

Humanistic psychology can be distinguished by a number of related characteristics. First, according to humanistic viewpoint, man's behaviour reflects more the operation of self-initiating tendencies than the influence of external factors. In other words, individuals are basically self-determining, rational and active in shaping their own growth and environments rather than passive reactors to the conditions of their upbringing and the social forces that impinge upon them. Secondly, conscious rationality, intents and decision-making characterize human behaviour more than irrationality of uncontrollable, unconscious impulses. Thirdly, humanistic psychology places emphasis on man's uniqueness, both as an individual and as a species. A fourth characteristic of humanistic psychology is its accent on man's future orientation, his continuing sense of purpose and his tendency toward psychological growth. Furthermore, humanistic psychologist stress "the spirit of man" and his brotherhood with all men. They are quite tolerant of amibguity. They are keenly interested in the study of the experience of the individual human being. They are essentially optimistic with the assumption that natural man is good and is capable of self-direction.

Humanistic psychology concerns itself with man in his wholeness. Its focus is on the individual as a whole and on the understanding of the person, not on the facts as such. Describing the essential characteristics of man when seen as a whole, various authors emphasize different points. Maslow (1965), for instance, stresses the aspects of "purposefulness" and of "Self-transcendence," May (1965) sees the main characteristic in man's having "intentionality" both in the sense of "meaning" and in the sense of "movement toward something." Rogers (1965), influenced by Polanyi, conceptualizes the wholeness as a "pattern of relationships" representing a "hidden reality." Although there are differences in the theories of these writers, their conceptions have a common tendency to de-emphasize such medical analogies as symptom reduction, cure or "adjustment."

The problem of the understanding of the person as a whole and in his whole course of life brought humanistic psychology into close relationship with existentialism. The experience of human existence is an essential basis to the humanistic thinking. May, Angel and Evenberger (1958) have shown, in penetrating studies, the relevance of existentialism to humanistic psychology as well as to humanistic psychotherapy. The essential goal of the humanistic psychotherapist is to help the person experience his existence as real.

Thus, humanistic psychology has successfully registered the restoration of the recognition that the inner life of man is as important psychologically as those elements in his behaviour which have been stressed by a radical empiricism in psychology. It addresses itself to the tasks of providing meaningful descriptions of this inner world, of exploring the inter-relationships among these aspects, keeping always within the context of the living, experiencing person and of inquiring into the further realms of possible experience which may be latent in each of us. Providing better conceptualizations, more inclusive theories, and more ingenious and adequate research techniques, humanistic psychology hopefully looks for epochal developments in the study of creativity and of ethical and aesthetic values. In short, humanistic psychology postulates a universe of infinite possibility.

Thanks to the advent of humanistic psychology, it is now possible to look upon man as a subject in the midst of his own living, acting on the world, changing himself and all about him. This fresh look puts greater emphasis on experience than on behaviour, on meaning than on causality, and on self-actualization than on other-manipulation. Man is, thus, seen in the evolution of his own possibilities or, in other words, in the process of "self-actualization." Thus, self-concept and the related constructs such as self-esteem and self-actualization become popular constructs within humanistic psychology around which a good deal of theorizing and empirical research has been attempted.

Self and self-actualization are essentially phenomenological constructs. The phenomenological viewpoint goes back at least to Adler (1930) who stressed self and consciousness in his "Individual Psychology." Consciousness of self and self-esteem form an integral part of Allport's (1950) conception of personality. Lacky (1951) treated the self as a unity which gives purpose and continuity to living. Sherif and Cantril (1947) brought in the term "ego-involvement" as a constellation of ego attitudes which "determine the more or less enduring character of one's personal identity." (p. 4) Hilgard (1949) proposed that the well-known mechanisms of adjustment imply a self-reference and are not understandable unless we adopt a concept of the self. The phenomenological view was featured even more by Snygg and Combs (1949) who stated that "all behavior without exception, is completely determined by and pertinent to the phenomenal field of the behaving organism." (p. 15)

Self-actualization is the most basic process among the mechanism used in maintaining and enhancing the self-concept. It denotes "full humanness" within the context of a growth psychology. In its simplest form, self-actualization is the process of becoming one's best and truest self. It implies progression through a sequential series of stages towards increasingly higher levels of motives and organization. It lays emphasis on constructive development of potential rather than concentration on obstacles to adjustment such as fear, anxiety and frustration. Self-actualization also implies a way of life compatible with one's unique pattern of traits and needs, instead of slavish imitation of others.

In brief, self-actualization theorists hold that all people are capable of reaching fulfilment, but the process demands knowledge, self-acceptance, full commitment, to a sense of mission and courage to pursue the mission regardless of pain. The process of unfolding the inner self and developing human potentiality demands that an individual, upon occasion, should reject conventional, cultural roles before he can trust his own judgment and develop his own potentiality.

Self-actualization is a key concept in the theories of Goldstein, Rogers and Maslow who saw man as striving for perfection and as actively engaged in the task of realizing his latent potential. For Goldstein (1939), self-actualization is at once the master motive and the creative aspect of man's life. For Rogers (1951), the human being has one basic tendency, namely, to actualize, maintain and enhance the experiencing organism. For Maslow (1954), the doctrine of self-actualization bridges the gulf between value and fact. Not only does Maslow share Nietzsche's concern about a non-theological basis for human values, but Nietzsche's Superman reappears in the guise of his self-actualizing person, the fully growing and self-fulfilling human being, the one in whom all his potentialities are coming to complete development and the one whose inner nature expresses itself freely, rather than being warped, suppressed or denied.

Thus, in the humanistic perspective, a self-actualizing person is conceptualized as less dependency- or deficiency-oriented than either the inner- or other-directed person. He could be characterized as having more of an autonomous, self-supportive or being orientation. He transcends complete inner-directedness by critical assimilation and creative expansion of his earlier principles of living. He discovers a mode of living which gives him confidence in himself. He tends to integrate the Freudian dichotomies and trichotomies. His impulses are more expressed and less controlled. His super ego is less harsh and punishing and less set off against his ego. The conative, the cognitive, the affective and the motor are less separated from each other and are more energetic in him. For him, there is no longer any distinction between selfishness and unselfishness, work and play, spirituality and sensuality and other such dichotomies. He is able to enjoy, to love, to laugh, to be humorous, to be whimsical and fantastic and to permit and enjoy emotional experiences, in general, and peak experiences in particular. He lives in the here and now more fully and is able to tie the past and the future to the present in meaningful continuity. He is less burdened by guilts, regrets and resentments, and his aspirations are linked meaningfully to the present working goals.

Although a good deal of theorizing has been undertaken and an elaborate account of the construct is available in psychological literature published in English language, it is surprising to note that not much of empirical work has been attempted on self-actualization. Except for Shostram's (1963) Personal Orientation Inventory which has been developed and used as a measure of self-actualization, we do not see any other significant attempt, especially in the East, to investigate empirically the concept of self-actualization. This book will investigate some important personality correlates of self-actualization by means of an empirical measure of self-actualization constructed for the purpose. As a background to the work, a detailed survey of the theory and available empirical research on the construct of self-actualization is reviewed in the following chapter.

Self-Actualization: A Review of Theory and Research

A. Theory of Self-Actualization

"When the philosophy of man changes," observes Maslow (1969), "then everything changes." We are now in the middle of such a change in the conception of man's capacities, potentialities and goals. There is now emerging over the horizon a new conception of human health and a new vision of possibilities of man and of his destiny. Most humanistic psychologists stress our positive nature—our push towards growth, fulfilment, actualization and the maintenance and enhancement of the organism.

1. Origins of Self-Actualization

True to his holistic viewpoint, Goldstein (1939) asserts that there is but one fundamental human motive—self-actualization—from which all other motives arise. According to him, hunger, thirst, the reproductive drive, the desire for knowledge, prestige and other primary and social motives are but manifestation of the basic tendency to realize the self. He feels that "coming to terms" with the environment and the maintenance of "constancy of the organism" are subservient to self-actualization. He believes that consistency and orderliness of behaviour in the phase of environmental change affords the best means of realizing the self. And he maintains that the organism does not seek only relief from annoying tensions and drives, but strives towards the goals of perfection. Thus, Goldstein holds that self-actualization, the fundamental human motive, is the source of all other motives, the satisfaction of which yields not just a release from tension but a positive joy in achievement and a pleasure in using one's potentialities.

Maslow (1964) does not consider self-actualization the source of all motivation but the highest form of motivation. Making a synthesis of holistic, motivational and cultural, approaches, Maslow proposes five degrees of need priority which lead to psychological health. He suggests that man has a number of primary instinctoid motives ranging from lower motives to higher ones. These are arranged in a hierarchy that corresponds to the assumed evolutionary level of the motive. First come the physiological motives like hunger, then the safety motives like fear, then the love motives, the esteem motives, and finally the motive for self-actualization. Progressing from the basic biological needs through the psychological needs, Maslow's hierarchy of needs culminates in needs for self-actualization. The hierarchy also refers to the order of the appearance of motives in the development of the individual—the physiological motives appear early, the safety and esteem ones later, and the needs for self-actualization much later, if at all.

Maslow's Theory of Needs

(a) The Physiological Needs

The most prepotent of all human needs are the physiological drives or needs. When the organism is dominated by the physiological needs such as hunger, thirst and sexual appetite, all other needs may become simply non-existent or will be pushed into the background. For instance, for the man who is extremely hungry, no other interests exist but food. His emotions, perceptions, thought processes and behaviour in general are preoccupied solely with getting food. As Maslow (1954) puts it, "he dreams food, he remembers food, he thinks about food, he emotes only about food, he perceives only food and he wants only food." Similarly, the sexually-deprived individual is over driven by sexual desire; other considerations become unimportant in the light of this overwhelming need.

(b) The Safety Needs

If the physiological needs are relatively well-gratified, there then emerges a new set of needs which may roughly be categorized as the safety needs. Maslow believes that the safety needs are most readily observable in the child because of its relative helplessness and dependence on adults. In the healthy, normal and fortunate adult, the safety needs are largely satisfied in our culture. The peaceful, smoothly running, good society ordinarily makes its members feel safe enough from wild animals, criminal assault, murder and tyranny. Therefore, in a very real sense, he no longer has any safety needs as active motivators, just as a sated man no longer feels hungry and a safe man no longer feels endangered. If we wish to perceive safety needs directly and clearly, we must turn to neurotic or near-neurotic individuals and to the economic and social underdogs. In between these extremes, we can perceive the expression of safety needs only in such phenomena as the common preference for a permanent job, the desire for a saving account and for insurance of various kinds—medical, unemployment, disability and old age.

(c) The Belongingness and Love Needs

If both the physiological and safety needs are fairly well-gratified, there will emerge the love and affection and belongingness needs. Now, the person will feel keenly the absence of friends or a sweet-heart or wife or children. He will hunger for affectionate relations with people in general. The thwarting of those needs results in maladjustment and severe psychopathology. Love is not synonymous with sex. It should also be noted that love needs involve both giving and receiving love.

(d) The Esteem Needs

With a few pathological exceptions, all people have a need or desire for self-respect or self-esteem and for the esteem of others. These needs may be classified into two sets. First, we have the desire for strength, for achievement, for adequacy, for competence and confidence, and for independence and freedom. Second, we have the desire for reputation and prestige, status, dominance, recognition, attention, importance or appreciation. Satisfaction of these self-esteem needs leads to feeling of self-confidence, worth, strength and capability. But, thwarting of these needs produces feelings of inferiority, of weakness and of helplessness which, in turn, give rise to basic discouragement or neurotic trends.

(e) The Need for Self-Actualization

At the top of the motivational pyramid lie the self-actualization needs. Even if all the needs—physiological, safety, love and belongingness and esteem—are satisfied, a new discontent and restlessness will soon develop unless the individual is doing what he is fitted for. The musician must create music, the artist must paint and the poet must compose if he is to be ultimately at peace with himself. As Maslow (1954) says, "what a man can be, he must be." This need is called self-actualization which emerges usually after the prior satisfaction of the physiological, safety, love and esteem needs.

In explaining the five needs, Maslow feels that achieving one level drives a person on to the next higher level. However, an unsatisfied need at the lower end of the hierarchy will inhibit the higher need. Maslow believes that the first two levels have been highly over-empathized by most personality theories. The ultimate and achievable nature of man is to operate at the upper levels, and especially at the self-actualization level. It is quite possible that at times society inhibits man's striving to actualize himself. Maslow's point is that human behaviour is not a question of normality or dichotomy between good and bad behaviour, but is essentially a question of self-fulfilment. Thus, what is normal is not a comparative thing but an inner ability to make oneself the best and the fullest possible personality that he or she is able to create.

(f) Degrees of Relative Satisfaction

The theoretical discussion of these five sets of basic needs may give a false impression that a need must necessarily be satisfied 100 percent before the next need emerges. But in actual practice, most members of our society, who are normal, are partially satisfied and partially unsatisfied in their needs at the same time. A more realistic description of hierarchy would, therefore, be in terms of decreasing percentage of satisfaction as we group a hierarchy of prepotency. The average citizen is satisfied 85 per cent in his physiological needs, 70 per cent in his safety needs, 50 per cent in his love needs, 40 per cent in his self-esteem needs and 10 per cent in his self-actualization needs. (Maslow, 1954)

(g) Reversal of the Hierarchy

The degree of the hierarchy of the basic needs is, however, not rigid. For instance, there are people in whom self-esteem seems to be more important than love. There are other people in whom the drive to create is more important than any other motive. More important than all these exceptions are the people who have high values, ideals and high social standards. With such values, they become martyrs. They will give up everything for the sake of an ideal or value.

Maslow considers that independent of his hierarchy of needs are motivational tendencies towards independence and individual achievement which may transcend at the stage of self-actualization. Many conflicts in life arise from independence and achievement motivation. And Maslow (1954) admits that although reasonable satisfaction of lower needs may be a pre-requisite for the attainment of self-actualization, there must be the capacity to overcome frustration and conflicts. But it must be through realizations and acceptance, not through escape and avoidance. Thus, self-actualization cannot be attributed to individuals in whom an over-riding interest is joined with avoidance or repression of emotional difficulties and problems of social relationship. So, in self-actualization, there must be a harmonization of motivation relating to interest, personal achievement and involvement in human relationships which is found in the truly great.

2. The Concept of Self-Actualization

Thus, self-actualization is a recent construct in psychology. It is generally posited as a central unitary motivating force that impels human behaviour and determines the course of development and expression of human personality.

It was coined by Goldstein (1939) as a protest against analyzing the organism into small bits, thus losing sight of the whole—the integrated and organized personality. Since then, the concept has become an important part of the psychological language. It became a vital part of the theories of a number of humanistically oriented psychologists such as Fromm (1947), Snygg and Combs (1949), Cantril (1950), Maslow (1954), Allport (1955), Murphy (1958), Erickson (1959), May (1961), Rogers (1961), Buhler (1962), and Bertalanffy (1965).

Self-actualization is hard enough to define. Perhaps, its meaning could be indicated rather than defined partly by positive pointing and partly by negative contrast. Self-actualization does not mean doing some far out thing necessarily, but going through an arduous and demanding period of preparation in order to realize one's possibilities. It means working to do well the thing that one wants to do. It is experiencing fully, vividly, selflessly with full concentration and total absorption. Also, self-actualization is not something extrinsic to the organism that the organism needs for health. It is an intrinsic growth of what is already in the organism. In other words, self-actualization is growing from within rather than being shaped from without.

Goldstein (1939) considers self-actualization the master motive and the creative aspect of man's life. He argues that all fundamental habit mechanisms arise out of an innate impulse to grow and realize potential hereditary capacities. He identifies this fundamental impulse, to grow and develop as the "tendency to perfection."

In his client-centered approach to psychotherapy, Rogers (1961) spells out that everyone has, within himself, a positive striving to become that of which he is capable. He feels that the basic force motivating the human organism is self-actualization which he defines as "a tendency towards fulfilment, towards actualization, towards the maintenance and enhancement of the organism." As the organism grows, it seeks to fulfil its potential within the limits of its heredity. A person may not always clearly perceive those actions that lead to growth and those that are regressive. But once he knows, he invariably chooses to grow rather than to regress.

It is Maslow (1954) who has developed the concept of self-actualization most thoroughly in his monumental study of self-actualizing people. In his words, self-actualization "refers to man's desire for self-fulfilment, namely, to the tendency to become actualized in what he is potentially. This tendency might be phrased as the desire to become more and more what one is, to become everything that one is capable of becoming." Thus, self-actualization is the full use and exploitation of talents, capacities and latent potentialities. Self-actualization may be summed up in Nietzsche's exhortation, "become what thou art." In his attempt to enlarge the scope of self-actualization so as to purge it of its static, all typological shortcomings, Maslow (1968) redefines self-actualization as "an episode, or a spurt in which the powers of the person come together in a particularly efficient and intensely enjoyable way and in which he is more integrated and less split, more open for experience, more idiosyncratic, more perfectly expressive or spontaneous, or fully functioning, more creative, more humorous, more ego-transcending, more independent of his lower need, etc. He becomes in these episodes more truly himself, more perfectly actualizing his potentialities, closer to the core of his Being, more fully human." (p. 97)

Self-actualization is, thus, defined in various ways, but a solid core of agreement is perceptible. As Maslow (1968) puts it, "all definitions accept or imply (a) acceptance and expression of the inner core or self, i.e. actualization of these latent capacities , and potentialities 'full functioning,' availability of the human and personal essence. (b) They all imply minimal presence of ill health, neurosis, psychosis, or loss of diminution of the basic human and personal capacities." (p. 197)

Thus, humanistic writers emphasize that self-actualization is a continuous process of growth towards greater fulfilment of one's potentials and that healthy persons achieve a better understanding of both themselves and the world. A self-actualizing person in comparison with an individual lacking in self-actualization is conceptualized as one who utilizes his talents and capabilities more fully, uses time effectively, functions relatively autonomously, tends to live in the present and has a more benevolent outlook on life and on human nature.

In conclusion, it should be noted that self-actualization is a relatively achieved "state of affairs" in a few people. In most people, however, it is rather a hope, a yearning, a drive, a "something" wished for but not yet achieved, showing itself clinically as drive towards health, integration and growth. Self-actualization values exist as goals and are real even though not yet actualized.

3. Pre-Requisites of Self-Actualization

(a) Acceptance of Essential Inner Nature

Self-actualization is possible only when the essential inner nature of man is fundamentally accepted, loved and respected. We have, each one of us, an essential biologically based inner nature which is instinctoid, intrinsic, given and natural with appreciable hereditary determinants. This essential inner nature includes instinctoid basic needs, capacities, talents, physiological or temperamental balances, prenatal and natal injuries. Each person's inner nature is partly unique to himself and partly species-wide. This inner nature does not seem to be intrinsically evil, but either neutral or positively good. If this essential core of the person is denied or suppressed, he gets sick. If, on the other hand, it is permitted to guide his life he grows healthy, fruitful and happy. However, the inner nature is not strong and overpowering, but "weak, delicate and subtle," and hence it is easily overcome by faulty habits, cultural pressure, bad parents and wrong attitudes to it. Even though weak, it rarely disappears in the normal person. Even though denied, the inner nature "persists underground forever pressing for actualization." (Moustakes, 1956, p. 233)

(b) Capacities as Needs

To make self-actualization possible, it is also necessary to understand that capacities, talents, organs or organ systems press to function and to be used and exercised. It is imperative to know that such use of capacities and organs is satisfying and disuse irritating. For instance, the muscular person likes to use his muscles. He has got to use them in order to "feel good." So also for the capacity to live. As Maslow (1962) puts it, "capacities clamour to be used and cease clamour only when they are well used." In this sense, capacities are also needs. The unused capacity or skill can become a diseased centre and diminish the person. Hence, it is best to bring out and encourage one's capacities, talents, potentialities rather than to suppress or repress them.

(c) Growth Motivation instead of Deficiency Motivation

For an adequate realization of one's potentialities one must have a "growth motivation," instead of "deficiency motivation." (Maslow, 1955) Deficiency motivation is the gratification of basic needs such as safety, belongingness, love, respect and self-esteem which are essentially deficits in the organism, empty holes which must be filled up for health's sake from within by human beings other than the subject. Growth motivation is the fulfilment of talents, capacities, creative tendencies and constitutional potentialities. Satisfying deficiencies only avoids illness. Growth satisfactions produce positive health. Healthy people have their basic needs for safety, belongingness, love, respect and self-esteem sufficiently gratified so much so that they are motivated primarily by trends towards self-actualization as a fuller knowledge and acceptance of the person's own intrinsic nature.

(d) Dropping Away of the Childhood Techniques

There is another pre-requisite for self-actualization, namely, dropping away of the techniques used by the child in his weakness and smallness for adapting himself to the strong, large, all-powerful, God-like adults. The self-actualizing person must replace these techniques with the techniques of being strong and independent and of being a parent himself. This obviously involves giving up the child's desperate wish for the exclusive, total love of his parents while learning to love others. He must learn to gratify his own needs himself rather than depending upon the parents to gratify them. He must give up being good out of fear, and learn to be good because he wishes to be so. Also, he must discover his own conscience and give up his internalized parents as a sole ethical guide. Thus, by adapting these new techniques, the self-actualizing person replaces weakness with strength and fear with courage.

(e) A Framework of Values

Also, the self-actualizing person needs a framework of values, a philosophy of life to live by and understand, in the same sense that he needs sunlight, calcium or love. Maslow (1964) calls this "cognitive need to understand." Valuelessness results in value-illness and can become somatic illness as well. Hence, one needs a validated, usable system of human values that he can believe in and devote himself to. In one way or another, all self-actualizing people are to devote their lives to the search for what Maslow (1962) called the "being" values, the ultimate values which are intrinsic and cannot be reduced to anything more ultimate. These B-values include the truth and beauty and goodness of the ancients, and perfection, simplicity, comprehensiveness and several more.

4. Behaviours Leading to Self-Actualization

Let us now consider as to what self-actualization means in terms of actual behaviour. How to help ourselves move and grow towards self-actualization is a problem that engaged the attention of the psychologists of the "Third Force." Maslow (1967), who is deeply interested in helping people become more fully themselves, has suggested eight ways in which one self-actualizes.

(a) Experiencing without Self-Awareness

The first way to self-actualize is experiencing fully, vividly, selflessly with full concentration and total absorption without self-consciousness of the person concerned. At this moment when the self is actualizing itself, the person is wholly and fully human. We all experience such moments occasionally. The counsellors can help us to experience them more often and, what is more, they can encourage us to become totally absorbed in something and to forget our poses, our defences and our shyness.

(b) Making a Growth Choice rather than a Fear Choice

The second way to self-actualize is to make a growth choice instead of a fear choice. Life is a process of choices. At each point, there is a progression or growth choice and a regression or fear choice. For instance, to choose to be honest instead of lying at a particular point is to make a growth choice. But moving towards defences, towards safety and towards being afraid is a fear choice. The more the number of growth choices, the quicker the pace towards self-actualization.

(c) Listening to the Impulse Voices

A human being is not a "tabula rasa," but with a self to be actualized. He has his own temperament, his own impulses with their voices. Generally, we listen not to ourselves, but to the voices of our parents and elders or to the voice of authority and tradition. It is by allowing ourselves to listen to the "impulse voices," the "Supreme Court" inside ourselves, and not simply to the voice of others, however strong they are, that we would be letting the self emerge, thereby moving towards self-actualization.

(d) Being Honest and Taking Responsibility

The fourth step towards self-actualization is being honest and taking responsibility. Frequently we are not honest when we are in doubt. We play games. Instead of admitting our ignorance frankly, we pretend and pose. What, instead, we should do is to look within ourselves for many of the answers to the various questions posed in life. We should freely and frankly admit our limitations and pitfalls and take the due responsibility. Each time one takes responsibility, his self is actualizing itself.

(e) Being True to Oneself

One should be true to oneself in order to move towards self-actualization. "Above all, be true to thy own self," says Shakespeare through Polonius in *Hamlet.* At each moment in life, one should say or do what he innately feels like saying or doing. When the situation demands, one must be prepared to make a true statement thereby being bold enough to be different, unpopular and non-conformist. Unless one dares listen to one's own self and say calmly, "no, I do not like such and such," at each moment in life, one cannot choose wisely for a life. Thus, one should be courageous and even be prepared to be unpopular in order to self-actualize.

(f) Using One's Intelligence and Working Hard

Also, one should necessarily go through an arduous and demanding period of preparation, using one's possibilities and potentialities. Nothing towards self-actualization is possible without intelligence and hard work. One should use one's intelligence to the fullest extent and do the thing he wants to do as best as he can. For instance, to become a second-rate physician is not a good path to self-actualization. One should strive to be a first-rate physician or as good a physician as he can be.

(g) Having Peak Experiences

The process of self-actualization includes peak experiences, (Maslow, 1964) the moments of highest happiness and fulfilment which cannot be bought, guaranteed or even sought. The person in the peak experiences feels more integrated, more spontaneous, more expressive, more natural, more uncontrolled and freely flowing outward than at other times. He feels himself to be at the peak of his powers using all his capacities to the fullest and the best. Not only are these his happiest and most thrilling moments, but also moments of his greatest maturity, individuation and fulfilment. In a word, they are his healthiest moments. Although peak experience cannot be sought deliberately, "one can set up the conditions so that peak experiences are more likely." (Maslow, 1964) Though everyone has peak experiences at sometime or other, not everyone knows it. Nevertheless, metacounsellors can help recognize these little moments of ecstasy when they happen.

(h) Identifying Defences and Giving Them Up

Lastly, self-actualization involves finding out who one is, what he is, what he likes, what he does not like, what is good for him and what bad, and especially what his mission in life is. One can possibly do so only by identifying his defences and then finding the necessary courage to give them up. One of the defence mechanisms of an idealistic young man is that of "desacralizing" which means mistrusting of the possibilities of values and virtues of a person or thing. Self-actualization consists in giving up the defence mechanism of desacralizing and learning to "resacralize." Resacralizing means being willing to see a person under the aspect of eternity and being able to see the sacred, the eternal and the symbolic.

Thus, putting all these points together, we see that self-actualization is not a matter of one great moment, but a matter of degree and of frequency, thereby making it more amenable to available research procedures. Self-actualization need not be restricted to those rare subjects who may be said to be fulfilling themselves most of the time. As Maslow (1968) suggests, "in theory at least we may also search any life history for episodes of self-actualization; especially those of artists, intellectuals and other especially creative people, of profoundly religious people, and of people experiencing great insights in psychotherapy, or in other important growth experiences."

It has been observed that self-actualization is not altogether general and that it takes place via femaleness or maleness which are prepotent general-humanness (Maslow, 1968). This means that one must first be a healthy, femaleness-fulfilled woman or maleness-fulfilled man before self-actualization becomes possible. It is also observed that different constitutional types actualize themselves in different ways since they have different inner selves to actualize.

It is important to note that though self-actualization is easy in principle, it is very difficult to achieve in practice. By Maslowian criteria, only less than one per cent of the adult population achieves self-actualization. (Maslow, 1968) There are many reasons for this at various levels. One of the main reasons is the conviction that man's intrinsic nature is evil or dangerous. One biological determinant for the difficulty of achieving self-actualization is that human beings no longer have strong instincts which tell them unequivocally what to do, when, where and how. (Maslow, 1968)

Self-actualization, however, does not mean a transcendence of all human problems. Self-actualizing people are not altogether free from conflicts, anxiety, frustration, sadness, hurt and guilt. With increasing maturity, the self-actualizing person is confronted with the existential problems inherent in the nature of man even at his best. He may be troubled by an intrinsic conscience, if not by the Freudian super ego. Moreover, even though he has transcended the problems of Becoming, there remain the problems of Being.

Finally, paradoxically enough, the achievement of self-actualization ultimately means the transcendence of self itself and of self-consciousness and of selfishness. Self-actualization makes it easier for the person to be homonous, namely, to merge himself as a part in a larger whole than himself. (Angyal, 1941) Thus, with self-actualization, the person moves from "a low homonomy" to a "a high homonomy," from union downward to union upward, that is, from "a low Nirvana to a high Nirvana."

5. Characteristics of Self-Actualizing People

Maslow's main approach to self-actualization had been his study of those unusual people whom he considered to be composed of actualized, successful people possessing the ability to discover their own deepest roots of personality. With this framework, he came up with forty-nine people from public and private life. The list includes eminent historical figures those whom he considered to be self-actualizers—men and women who had made extraordinary use of their full potential and those living who, he believed, possessed the characteristics of good psychological health. Included in Maslow's group of self-actualizers were such persons as Abraham Lincoln, Thomas Jefferson, Walt Whitman, Thoreau, Roosevelt, Einstein, Schwetzer and a number of Maslow's friends and acquaintances and a few college students. After studying their lives, Maslow arrived at a composite picture of a self-actualizer. The distinguishing characteristics of self-actualizing persons are given below.

(a) More Efficient Perception of Reality

Self-actualizing people have an unusual ability to detect the spurious, the fake and dishonest in personality, and, in general, to judge people more correctly and efficiently than an average person. They are able to see concealed or confused realities more swiftly and more correctly than others in art and music, in political affairs, in things of the intellectual and scientific matters. They can distinguish far more easily than others the fresh, concrete and ideographic from the generic, abstract and rubricized. They live more in the real world of nature than in the man-made mass of concepts, expectations and beliefs. They have "the innocent eye" and, therefore, they are far more apt to perceive things as they are and not as they wish them to be. They are quite different from average man in being uniformly unthreatened and unfrightened by the unknown. They not only tolerate the ambiguous and unstructured but like it. In other words, they like the mysterious in life. Their predictions of the future are more often correct because they are less based upon wish, desire, anxiety, fear or optimism or pessimism.

(b) Acceptance of Self, Others and Nature

Self-actualizing people find it possible to accept themselves and their own nature without complaint. They can accept their own human nature in the stoic style, with all its shortcomings and with all its discrepancies from the ideal image. It does not, however, mean that they are self-satisfied. They can take the frailties and sins, weaknesses and evils of human nature into same unquestioning spirit with which one accepts the characteristics of nature. They see human nature as it is and not as they would prefer it to be. Their acceptance of self is at lower as well as at higher levels. They have a uniformly good appetite for food and they sleep well. They seem to enjoy their sexual lives without unnecessary inhibition. They are also able to accept themselves at higher levels—love, safety, belongingness and self-respect. They accept all of these without question as worthwhile, simply because they are inclined to accept the work of nature rather than to argue with her. They are free from cant, guile, hypocrisy and playing a game. They are not guilty of sex, pregnancy, menstruation and growing old, since they are part of reality. If at all they are guilty, they are guilty of improvable shortcomings, namely, laziness, loss of temper, hurting others, prejudice and jealousy. They feel bad about discrepancies between what is and what ought to be.

(c) Spontaneity

Self-actualizing people are spontaneous in their behaviour as well as in their inner life, thoughts and impulses. Their behaviour is marked by simplicity and naturalness and by the lack of artificiality or straining for effect. They are unconventional, but at the same time they do not like to hurt others. They will go through the ceremonies and rituals of conventions with a good-humoured shrug and with best possible grace. They have codes of ethics that are relatively autonomous and individual rather than conventional. They break conventions and laws when the situations demand it. It does not, however, mean that they are unethical. They are, in reality, the most ethical of people, even though their ethics are not necessarily the same as those of the people around them. If they behave in a conventional manner, it is either because no great issues are involved or because they do not like to embarrass others. They attempt to grow to perfection and to develop more and more fully in their own style. For them motivation is just character growth, character expression, maturation and development.

(d) Problem-Centered (Mission in Life)

Self-actualizing people have some mission in life, some tasks to fulfil and some problem outside themselves. The tasks they seek to fulfil are non-personal or unselfish, concerned with the good of mankind in general or of a nation in general. They are ordinarily concerned with basic issues and eternal questions pertaining to the philosophical or ethical. They work within a framework of values that are broad rather than petty, universal rather than local. They work in terms of a century rather than the moment. They are all, in one sense or another, philosophers.

(e) Detachment and Privacy

Almost all self-actualizing people positively like solitude and privacy to a greater degree than the average person. The introvert-extrovert dichotomy hardly applies to these people. They are essentially detached in life. They remain unruffled and undisturbed by that which produces turmoil in others. They find it easy to be aloof, reserved, calm and serene. It becomes possible for them to take personal misfortunes without reacting violently as the ordinary person does. They seem to be able to retain their dignity even in undignified surroundings and situations.

(f) Autonomy

Self-actualizing people are characterized by their relative independence of the physical and social environment. Since they are propelled by "growth motivation" rather than "deficiency motivation" they are not dependent on the real world or other people or culture for their main satisfactions. Instead, they depend on their own potentialities and latent resources for their own development. They can maintain a relative serenity and happiness in the midst of circumstances that would drive other people to suicide. They are relatively stable in the face of hard knocks, blows, deprivations, frustrations and the like. They are "self-contained." They are strong enough to be independent of the good and bad opinion of other people. The honours, the status, the rewards and the prestige they get from others are for them less important than self-development and inner growth.

(g) Continued Freshness of Appreciation

Self-actualizing people have the wonderful capacity to appreciate the basic goods of life freshly and naively, again and again with awe, pleasure and even ecstasy. They do not derive pleasure or inspiration by going to a night club or getting a lot of money or having a good time at a party. They get inspiration and strength from the basic experiences of life. They derive from sexual contacts the same kind of the basic strengthening and revivifying that other people derive from music or nature, not merely passing pleasure.

(h) Mystic Experience

The mystic experience is common for all self-actualizing people. Their mystic experiences, however, do not have any theological or supernatural reference. Their mystic experience is a natural experience, well within the jurisdiction of science. Their mystic experience is but a tremendous intensification of any of the experiences in which there is a loss of self or transcendence of self.

(i) Older-Brotherly Attitude (Gemeinschaftsgefuhl)

Self-actualizing people have a deep feeling of identification, sympathy and affection for human beings in general. They have a genuine desire to help the human race. It is as if they were all members of a single family. They are often saddened, exasperated and even enraged by the shortcomings of the average person. Nevertheless, they feel a basic underlying kinship with those people. They are truly interested in the welfare of man.

(j) Interpersonal Relations

Self-actualizing people have deeper and more profound interpersonal relations than any other adults. They are capable of more fusion, greater love, more obliteration of the ego-boundaries than other people. However, their love does not imply lack of discrimination. They do speak realistically and harshly of those who deserve it, especially of the hypocritical, the pretentious, the pompous and the self-inflated. They have deep and intimate relationship with rather few individuals. Their circle of friends is rather small. They are highly selective in friends. Their exclusiveness of devotion exists side by side with their widespreading benevolence, affection and friendliness. They tend to be kind or, at least, patient to almost everyone. They have an especially tender love for children and are easily touched by them. They had compassion for all mankind. They attract at least some admirers, friends, or even disciples or worshippers.

(k) Democratic Character Structure

All self-actualizing people, without exception, are democratic in the deepest possible sense. They can be friendly with anyone of suitable character irrespective of class, education, political belief, race or colour. They do not seem to be even aware of these differences which are so obvious and so important for the average person. They find it possible to learn from anybody who has something to teach them. In such a learning relationship, they do not try to maintain any outward dignity, status or age prestige. They are also quite humble. They are well aware of how little they know in comparison with what could be known and what is known by others. Because of this, they are honestly respectful and even humble before people who can teach them something that they do not know. They give this honest respect to a good carpenter who is a master of his craft. They are not, however, indiscriminating altogether in selecting friends. Themselves being elite, they select for their friends the elite, but this is an elite in character, capacity and talent rather than of birth, race, fame or power. They give certain quantum of respect to any human being just because he is a human individual.

(l) Discrimination between Means and Ends

Self-actualizing people have a clear notion of the difference between ends and means. They value and appreciate the means as much as they do the ends. So, they find as much pleasure and satisfaction in working toward a good as attaining it. They do not operate with rigid sets and prejudged methods. They can derive pleasure from even the most routine and apparently unchallenging tasks, like children. They are quite certain of their convictions. Unlike the average person, they do not show confusion, chaos and conflicting beliefs. They are ethical according to commonly accepted standards of conduct. To them, God is more a metaphysical concept than a personal figure. They are not religious in the formal sense of the term. Their religion is humanistic rather than theistic. They are essentially men of principles.

(m) Philosophical Sense of Humour

Self-actualizing people have a sense of humour which is not of the average type. They do not consider funny what the average man considers to be funny. Hence they do not derive laughter by hurting someone or from someone else's inferiority or by a rude joke. Their humour is thoughtful and philosophical, eliciting a smile rather than a laugh. They derive humour from human situation such as discrepancies between what is and what ought to be and peculiarities of things. They can laugh at their own shortcomings. Their humour often takes an educative or teaching role, but in the form of parables or fables. Their humour is spontaneous rather than planned and it can never be repeated.

(n) Creativeness

Creativeness is a universal characteristic of all self-actualizing people without exception. They seem to be specially endowed with a drive and capacity for this purpose. Each one shows in one way or another a special kind of creativeness or originality that has certain peculiar characteristics. This creativeness appears not in the usual forms of writing books, composing music or producing artistic objects, but in an expression of healthy personality. In this sense, there can be a creative shoe-maker or carpenter. The creativeness of the self-actualizing man seems rather to be akin to the naive and universal creativeness of unspoiled children.

(o) Resistance to Enculturation

Self-actualizing people tend to be non-conformists. They maintain a certain inner detachment from the culture they are immersed in. They may not outwardly differ from the culture in choice of clothes, language and food, but inwardly they differ radically. They follow their own norms of behaviour. They are conventional in superficial ways but are strongly self-determined. They would improve the culture from within, rather than reject it and fight it from without. They are autonomous in that they are ruled by their own characters rather than by the rules of society. They are less flattened out, less moulded and less dominated by the culture than the average people. They resist the harmful effects of their culture. They manage to get along by a complex combination of inner autonomy and outer acceptance.

The Imperfections of Self-Actualizing People

However good and admirable the self-actualizing people are, they have their own imperfections showing as they do many of the lesser human failings. They are not completely free from certain human weaknesses. They too are equipped with silly, wasteful or thoughtless habits. They can be boring, stubborn and irritating. They are also not completely free from superficial vanity, pride and partiality. They are subject to temper outbursts. They are capable of unexpected ruthlessness.

Also, in their concentration on some phenomenon or question, the self-actualizing people may become absent-minded or humourless and forget their ordinary social politeness. Even their kindness can lead them into mistakes, marrying out of pity, getting too closely involved with neurotics, allowing scoundrels to impose on them and encouraging parasites and psychopaths. They are also not fully free from guilt, anxiety, sadness, self-castigation, internal strife and conflict.

Thus, in a very modestly presented informal study, Maslow examines the characteristics of self-actualizing people who seem to him to exemplify or to approach the ideal of psychological health. And he talks about self-actualizing people as rare specimens of psychological health who can be used as a kind of touchstone to explore human potentialities.

From the humanistic perspective, the individual is also held to have what Fromm (1968) calls "transutilitarian" dimension. In addition to the drive to maximize utilities, people possess an inherent tendency towards increased personal autonomy and fulfillment of their capabilities. (Maslow, 1943; Rogers, 1965) Moreover, the rational, analytical side of human nature is balanced against an intuitive, holistic side which is of equal importance. (Deikman, 1971; Ornstein, 1972) Thus, self-actualization theory differs from the self-interested, rational actor model in two central respects: (a) "voluntaristic theory of multiple human needs, culminating in self-actualization replaces the deterministic, one-dimensional theory of utilitarianism and (b) the interaction of left-brain (rational) and right-brain (intuitive) modalities replaces bundles of preferences as an explanatory principle."

Self-actualization theory has some of its philosophical base in the work of the existential philosophers. Though basically self-actualization theory argues that man has a capability for a meaningful, viable, potential-filling existence, and that he has the properties and the nature to implement a meaningful existence, he has been prevented from engaging and behaving in this meaningful self-actualizing manner by the conditions and environments in which he lives. The role of the therapist is to understand the factors and conditions that are preventing man from reaching his self-actualizing state. He, then, tries to change these conditions so that man can reach the state in which his motivational processes will be towards self-actualization rather than toward some optimal motivation.

Although the concept of pseudo-self-actualization is potentially quite important, it has not developed theoretically or empirically beyond the level initially presented by Shostrom. As a result, it is difficult to define exact standards for judging pseudo-self-actualizing people or to determine its frequency. If, however, the concept is substantiated through empirical research and the proportion of pseudo-self-actualizers is high, then much of the previous research on self-actualization will have to be re-examined so as to determine to what extent the findings actually represent the behaviour of self-actualizers. (Forest and Siez, 1981)

6. A Critique of Self-Actualization Theory

Commenting on self-actualization theories, in general, Buhler (1959) notes that in spite of their vast superiority over homeostatic descriptions of motivation, a number of questions arise regarding the dynamics of the tendency towards self-fulfilment and its relation to the individual's biological "groundplan." The fundamental question she raises is whether self-actualization is a specific process or a name given to a whole group of processes. The question is pertinent if self-actualization is taken to mean the total development of the individual in an optimal way. Buhler also notes that even those who propose this theory do not seem to consider self-actualization as ultimate objective of human striving. In other words, the objective accomplishment of actualizing one's potential appears to be subservient to achieving a more basic goal—gratifying subjective experience.

Smith (1973) has dealt severely with several aspects of Maslow's doctrine of self-actualization. He notes a crucial flaw in what he calls "the boot-straps operation" by which Maslow selected his "sample" of self actualizing people. He argues that Maslow, in effect, eliminated people with gross pathology—the Dostoevskis and Van Goghs—and selected people for whom he had personally the highest admiration as human beings. In Smith's view, then, the characteristics of self-actualizing people must be regarded not as empirical description of the fully human but as an explication of his implicit conception of his orienting frame of human values.

Smith also feels that it is questionable to give as much weight as Maslow does to insights validated by the content of peak experiences which Maslow regards as transient moments of self-actualization. As peak experiences are on the non-rational, Dionysian side, Smith says that if one grants the co-reality of the more Appollonian forms of self-actualization, the authority of peak experiences diminishes and they figure less prominently as a characteristic of self-actualization.

Furthermore, Smith thinks that Maslow's doctrine of potentiality is more misleading than helpful. He says that Maslow's stretching of the biological analogy to cover the case of human psychology—"the environment does not give him (man) potentialities or capacities; he had them in inchoate or embryonic form, just as he has embryonic arms and legs" (p. 160)—will hardly do. He is of the view that human potentialities are not "built-in" but exist as possibilities among a range of very different ones.

Goble (1974) finds Smith's principal argument in his essay on self-actualization "irrefutable." He is also of the view that "Maslow's concept of self-actualization is suspect—not "scientific"—because it was based on his subjective vision of the definition of mental health." (p. 75) He feels that Maslow made value judgements in his selection of self-actualizers and that he was not justified in excluding Stalin or Napoleon from his selection of self-actualizing people.

Antsyferova (1973) questions Maslow's views on personality need hierarchy and self-actualization. While his positive contributions are acknowledged, his placing of the source of self-actualization entirely within the individual, the ignoring of societal development and its determining role in personality formation and his misinterpretation of the relationship between society and the individual are severely criticized.

Slepova (1976) presents a critique of the idea of self-actualization in the works of Allport and Maslow while recognizing as positive such features of humanistic psychology as the emphasis on the importance of self-actualization and the individual nature of personality development, both Allport's and Maslow's conceptualizations of the nature and development of personality are seen as fundamentally idealistic. These conceptualizations, according to the author, do not answer the question of the nature of self-actualization or the way an individual acquires authentic freedom.

Aron (1977) suggests that Maslow's theoretical framework disregards political and ethical concerns and that this is due to his lack of a coherent theory of self-development. He says that the dominant social pattern of the hippie movement, in its early days, was based on notions that could be identified as similar to Maslow's. Therefore, he argues that the hippies, whether or not they knew it, were Maslovians and it became legitimate to regard interpersonal hippie problems as resulting from contradictions within Maslow's theory. Maslow, in Aron's view, failed to deal consistently with the self-society relationship. He had two irreconcilable views of the self—as sovereign and inviolable on the one hand, and as unequal ("some people make better choices") on the other. He concludes that contradiction between what may be called democratic and aristocratic premises resulted in the moral paralysis of the hippies who tried to live according to both of these principles.

Hampden (1977), in a rejoinder to Aron's criticism of Maslow's theory, says that Aron's critique of Maslow is largely a critique of Aron's personal conception of Maslow's theory. He rightly points out that Maslow did not think in terms of polarities and his theory cannot properly be phrased in those terms. Thus, Aron's major assumption that equality and authority are irreconcilably opposed is shown to be a fallacy.

Buss (1979) opines that one can understand the liberal, ideological foundation of Maslow's theory from self-actualization by giving it a critical and dialectical reading. He says that, ideologically speaking, the validity of Maslow's theory derives from the contradictory social reality it reflects and supports—a two-class theory of individual freedom and development. However, Maslow's theory is, at the same time, an inversion of that reality to the extent that its psychological categoires universalize an historically specific conditon, namely, democractic eliticism.

Geller (1982) critically examines the self-actualization theories of Rogers and Maslow. He argues that neither theory is correct. The fundamental claims of each, especially about the self and the human conditions, are shown to be radically mistaken. According to him, Rogers's theory is unacceptable insofar as his conception of the touchstone or standards of self-actualization is false, incoherent and unworkable in practice. He says that Maslow's theory must be rejected because of an inadequate anthropodicy (theory of evil) and ontology. He contends that Maslow's explanation of one major form of human diminution, what he calls the "metapathologies" of contemporary life, undermines the normative foundations of his theory. Secondly, the logic of human development upon which the entire edifice of Maslow's theory rests is shown to be essentially reductionist and radically mistaken. Because of his commitment to a reductionist logic, Maslow is unable in principle to offer an adequate account of the origin and nature of the self and human needs. Geller concludes his provocative study by presuming that self-actualization theory as such has very little to offer towards understanding and improving the human condition within late twentieth-century Western society.

Frick (1982) questions Maslow's theory that progressive gratification through the need hierarchy would lead individuals automatically to explore their higher needs for self-actualization. He says that Maslow himself came to realize later that many did not move towards self-actualization even after all other needs in the hierarchy had been gratified. This discovery necessitated a rethinking of Maslow's theory. A crucial element in his theory is that self-actualization, the highest need in the hierarchy, is the weakest biologically. This led Frick to believe that self-actualization requires some auxiliary source of strength and support. Thus, he develops the thesis that strong conceptual support provided by growth-enhancing concepts is an essential variable for achieving self-actualization.

B. Empirical Research

The notion of self has staged a dramatic comeback during the Forties after having been in a state of animated suspension for a part of the present century under the cramping impact of behavioristic, positivistic onslaught. Thanks to Rogerian non-directive client-centered therapy with its dictum that "every individual exists in a continually changing world of experience of which he is the centre,"

(1951, p. 483) projecting the view that "the best vantage point for understanding behaviour is from the internal frame of reference of the individual himself," (p. 494) there has been a resurgence of interest among psychologists in the concept of the self. Today self stands naked for all to examine, evaluate, theorize about and to make empirical investigation.

Concerned with the subjective experience and expansion of human possibilities, the concept of self-actualization has a tremendous range of available methods for its study. All the fields of study—philosophy, religion, history, literature, art and many other areas, by which man has from the earliest times tried to inquire into his own nature and destiny—are available for its work. Physiological observations as well as philosophical analysis, biological deductions as well as introspection and contemplation, reasoning as well as mystical insight—all these and even more possible tools of the tasks—have been employed by the humanistic psychologists to study various aspects of self-actualization.

The last four decades (1940-1980) could be viewed as the era of self-actualization for the concept of self itself. The first of these decades could be looked upon as the period of theorizing, the second was the decade of intense research activity, and the third and fourth could be considered the decade of criticism and consolidation.

It is said that the value of a good theory consists in stimulating and promoting research. If it is so, one is compelled to state that the theory of self-actualization has more than fulfilled this expectation in terms of the number and variety of research it has stimulated. Actually, there has been a deluge of studies. To review all the published literature on self-actualization is a tremendous task, and it is beyond the scope of the present book. However, an attempt is made in the following pages to review some of the outstanding works in the field.

1. The Beginnings of Self-Actualization Studies

It is at once interesting and important to note that investigations on self-actualization were not planned to be research and naturally did not start out as research. They started out, instead, as the efforts of a young intellectual, Abraham Maslow, to try to understand two of his teachers, Ruth Benedict, a renowned anthropologist, and May Wortheimer, a great gestalt psychologist, whom he loved, admired and adored, and who were very "wonderful" people in themselves. Maslow was not content to simply adore them, but wanted to understand why those two people were so different from the "run-of-the-mill" people in the world.

Maslow's investigation began as a pre-scientific or non-scientific activity. He made notes on Wortheimer and Benedict. When he tried to understand them, think about them and write about them in his journal, he realized in one "wonderful moment" that their two patterns could be generalized. It was, indeed, an exciting experience for Maslow. He tried to see whether the pattern of the two teachers could be found elsewhere. And he was able to find such a pattern elsewhere, in one person after another.

Maslow selected some two dozen people whom he liked or admired very much and then tried to figure them out and found that he was able to describe a syndrome—the kind of pattern that seemed to fit all of them. He made some generalizations which grew out of his selection of certain kinds of people. By ordinary standards of laboratory research, this was simply not research at all. But, one should bear in mind that this was not planned as an ordinary research. It was not a social venture but a private one, motivated by Maslow's own curiosity and pointed towards the solution of various personal, moral, ethical and scientific problems. He sought only to convince and to teach himself rather than to prove or to demonstrate to others. (Maslow, 1954) Instead of writing for conventionally reliable data, Maslow plunged in without fearing mistakes to do the best he could, hoping to learn enough from blunders and to correct them eventually.

The subjects for Maslow's investigation were selected from among his personal acquaintances and friends, and from among public and historical figures. In addition, in a first research with young people, 3000 college students were screened, but yielded only one immediately usable subject and a dozen or two possible future subjects. From his study of college students, Maslow found that the sort of self-actualization he had noticed in his older subjects was not possible for young, developing people. It was also felt that characters created by novelists or dramatists could also be used for demonstration purposes. Though a thought-provoking finding in itself, it did not yield any positive results as none were found that were usable in his culture and time.

The first clinical definition of self-actualization, on the basis of which subjects were finally chosen or rejected, had a positive as well as a negative side. The negative criterion was absence of neurosis, psychopathic personality and psychosis, or strong tendencies in that direction. The positive criterion for selection of people was positive evidence of self-actualization—the full use and exploitation of talents, capacities and potentialities. They are the people who have developed or are developing to the full stature of which they are capable.

The criterion for selection of subjects also implied gratification of the basic emotional needs for safety, belongingness, love, respect and self-respect, and of the cognitive needs for knowledge and understanding or, in a few cases, conquest of these needs. Maslow's (1954) statement in this context is noteworthy: "it is still an open question as to whether this basic gratification is a sufficient or only a pre-requisite condition of self-actualization. It may be that self-actualization means basic gratification plus at least minimum talents, capacity or richness."

Maslow's technique of selection of subjects for his investigation was that of iteration, previously used in studies of the personality syndromes of self-esteem and of security. This consists in starting with the personal or cultural non-technical state of belief, collating the various extent usages and definitions of the syndrome, and then defining it more carefully, still in terms of actual usage, eliminating the logical and factual inconsistencies, usually found in folk definitions.

On the basis of the corrected folk definition, the first groups of subjects, who were high as well as low in the quality, were selected. These people were studied as carefully as possible in the clinical style, and on the basis of this empirical study the original corrected folk definition was further changed and corrected as required by the data now in hand. This gave the first clinical definition of self-actualization. On the basis of this new definition, the original group of subjects was reselected, some being retained and some being dropped and some new ones being added. This second level group of subjects was then in its turn experimentally and statistically studied causing modification, correction and enrichment of the first clinical definition with which in turn a new group of subjects was selected and so on and so forth. In this way, an ordinary vague and unscientific folk concept of self-actualization became more and more exact, more and more operational in character and, therefore, more scientific.

Because of the various limitations under which Maslow had to conduct his study of self-actualizing people—the small number of subjects as well as incompleteness of the data—no quantitative presentation of self-actualizing people was made possible. Only "composite impressions" could be offered for whatever they might be worth. And the holistic analysis of these total impressions yielded some important and useful characteristics of self-actualizing people for further clinical and experimental study.

After Maslow published the result of his investigations, there appeared several lines of evidence that supported his findings, not by replication, but by approaches from different angles. Rogers's findings (1961) and those of his students added up to corroboration for the whole syndrome of self-actualization. Bugental (1965) has offered confirmatory evidence from psychotherapy. Some of the new work with LSD, (Mogar, 1967) and some of the studies on the effects of therapy (Strupp, 1960; Frank, 1961; Goldstein,

1962; Shapiro, 1964; Unger, 1964, Mogar, 1965a) also add upto corroborative support for Maslow's study.

2. Self-Actualization and the Group Experience

There seems to be an intense need for modern man to find meaning in his existence not only by actualizing potential for living fully, but also by relating himself at deep and significant levels to others. To enable this to occur, a number of studies have reported ways of providing settings and meeting certain conditions.

Thomas (1968) shows that it is possible to establish a group climate which, in a relatively brief period of time, seems to facilitate a heightened state of being somewhat similar in nature to the experiences of the fully functioning person depicted by Rogers (1961) and the self-actualizing person described by Maslow (1954). He states that the concepts of "fully functioning" and "self-actualized" apply not only to fully functioning or self-actualized people, but also to states of being which can be attained at a given moment in time by many people, provided certain conditions are met. On the basis of his own personal involvement in a couple of fairly intensive group experiences which were three full days in length, Thomas spells out the conditions necessary for facilitating a group experience. The basic encounter group consisting of about twelve to fifteen members plus two experienced group leaders should have the opportunity to meet together for approximately two or three two-hour sessions daily for several days and live together in a setting which enables them to be removed from the usual distractions of work, family and social pressure. Thomas is convinced that when the individual is able to surrender himself to this process and move into the situation, maintaining as much openness as possible, genuine growth will occur. It is possible to experience the state of Rogers's fully functioning person, and one who has experienced this state knows that the act of living fully, although it involves considerable risk, is preferable. Another important feature of such group experiences is that in a relatively short period of time people find themselves able to rely less on the past and to live more in the present moment.

Treppa and Fricke (1972) examined effects from weekend marathon group experience on values of self-actualization and on the interpersonal dimension of personality. A total of twenty-two undergraduate volunteers were given the Personal Orientation Inventory, MMPI and Interpersonal checklist, immediately before experimental subjects participated in the marathon group, two days after, and six weeks later. Both experimental and control subjects showed significantly positive changes on post-test and follow-up scores. It was concluded that previous investigators were premature in believing in the positive effects of marathon group experience. Results suggested the hypothesis that subjects who volunteer for a marathon group may become more self-actualized through expression of this need, whether or not they actually experience the group and that repeated testing may account for the positive change in both groups.

Kilmann, Sotile and Fritz (1978) investigated the comparative ability of a marathon and a weekly encounter group to produce gains in self-actualization by administering the POI. The subjects were twenty-three undergraduates who volunteered for each of the experiences. The marathon group was conducted for sixteen continuous hours. The weekly group met for two hours, twice weekly, for four weeks. Both treatment groups, conducted by the same leader, received the same sequence of group exercises. A significant group effect indicated that both groups increased their self-actualization scores from the pre-tests. No significant differences were found between the two experimental groups on self-actualization or perceived adjustment to life events over the two year follow-up.

Kilmann et al, (1976) investigated the impact of a sixteen-hour marathon session on levels of self-actualization and attitudes toward women (as measured by Personal Orientation Inventory and the Attitudes Toward Women Scale) both one day and five weeks after the group experiences. Twenty-eight female undergraduates were randomly assigned to one of two marathon groups or to a no-treatment control group. Subjects in both marathon groups experienced a significant shift toward increased independence or self-supportedness on both post-tests. However, subjects in one marathon group reflected significantly greater agreement with pro-feminist attitudes on the first post-test and experienced an even greater shifts in that direction on the second post-test, while subjects in the other marathon group did not differ significantly from controls on either post-test. Leader variables may account for these results.

Ott and Geyer (1972) reported experiences of self-actualization group consisting of eight members of the medical and psychological staff of a neuropsychiatric clinic. The group met for ninety minutes a week for eighteen months. Problems of being a group leader and a participant were discussed including those which occurred when all group members were employed by the same institution. The group proved to be a controlled method for improving psychotherapy as well as training in group therapy. It was found that the group experience elevated the patients discussed, from objects of therapy to partners of the therapist.

Johnson and Johnson (1979) studied forty graduate counselling students who were randomly assigned by sex to a marathon group (two eight-hour sessions), a shorter session group (eight two-hour sessions), a combination of marathon and shorter session group (one eight-hour and four two-hour sessions) and a control group to determine the impact of growth groups on the self-actualization of participants. The POI, which was administered to all the subjects before and after the group experience, indicated some significant positive movement for treatment groups. However, no single approach was found to be significantly more effective than the others.

Peteroy (1979) studies the effects of member and leader expectations on group members, self-actualization and self-esteem gain. The change in self-acutalization and self-esteem between experimental groups and a non-treatment comparison group also were asssessed. The subjects for experimental groups were forty-two University students enrolled in an introductory group counselling courses. All students participated twice weekly as members of a growth group (three hours per week) for twenty-five sessions. Thirty-one students from a different class served as a non-treatment group. Leaders for the experiment group were six advanced graduate students in counselling psychology. Members and leaders were assigned randomly to groups on the basis of an expectation scale with three types of member groups (high, moderate, low) being facilitated by high and low expectation leaders. Results indicated that varying the level of group expectations did not significantly affect self-actualization gain but did affect self-esteem change. Significant differences were also found between the experimental and control groups on the dependent variables.

In short, studies on self-actualization in relation to group experience indicate that it is possible to apply the concepts of Rogers's "fully functioning person" and Maslow's "self-actualizing person" to states of being which can be attained by many people at a given moment by meeting certain conditions. It is suggested that people who volunteer for a marathon group may become more self-actualized. The subjects in a marathon group experienced a significant shift towards increased independence or self-supportedness. It was also found that the group experience elevates the participants from the objects of therapy to partners of the therapists.

3. Self-Actualization and Students

Self-actualization has been studied among students with references to their academic achievement, capacity to adjustment, socio-economic status and their occupational prestige aspirations. Some recent investigations on self-actualization have concerned themselves with exploring the effects of dogmatism on the self-actualization of students as well as the effect of counsellor-induced conditions of the present-centeredness on self-actualization in college students.

Knott (1975) explored the nature of relationship between academic achievement and self-actualization, from the viewpoint of prior measure of self-actualization, taking 278 students as subjects. Sex and ability level were also tested as additional independent variables over the eight repeated measures. The two-way analysis of variance was used to test differences between groups and for interaction effects for purposes of grouping. The subjects were categorized into two ability groups with combined SAT scores, 1001 defining the high ability group, and scores totalling 1000 or less determining the low ability group. The results indicated that there were no significant differences in academic achievement between levels of self-actualization when compared over the full eight semesters's undergraduate experience. However, there was a significant (p. 5) interaction effect found for self-actualization over the eight semester on GPA attainment, although low self-actualized entrants achieved higher overall grade levels. Ability was also significantly related to academic achievement (p. 1) but sex and other combinations of the variables measured did not interact significantly.

Kiss (1975) conducted a study to ascertain the existence of distinctive personality patterns related to sociometric status among high school students. The personality measures of interest to the study were those of self-actualization as measured by the POI, and those of adjustment by the MCI (Minnesota Counselling Inventory). The subjects were 461 junior and senior students attending a Catholic Regional High School. The most remarkable comment that could be made about the finding on adjustment was that students, regardless of the sociometric status which they held along with their peers, did not differ in how well or poorly they are adjusting to their families, school or themselves. In terms of self-actualization, the findings seemed to indicate that self-actualizing values were least developed for the highly rejected group. Girls appear to have a slight edge over boys in the direction of better adjustment and more mature self-actualizing values.

Harringan (1975) investigated the comparative effects of a 16-hour and 24-hour marathon Gestalt workshop on an overall measure of self-actualization of 32 volunteer growth seeking college students. Both immediate and long-term effects were examined. Secondly, the investigation explored the effect of dogmatics, as measured by the Rokeach Dogmatism Scale, on marathon participants's changes in measured self-actualization. Each participant completed the RDS at the conclusion of a workshop screening interview. The subjects were divided into two groups—High and Low, according to their Dogmatism scores and subjects in each group were then randomly assigned to either a 16-hour or a 24-hour marathon Gestalt workshop. The participants completed the POI before, after and 8-weeks following the workshops. The findings of the study demonstrated that both the 16-hour and the 24-hour marathon Gestalt workshops appear to foster the increased self-actualization of volunteer college student participants. Further, it appears that positive gains in self-actualization remain stable over an eight week follow-up period. The participants's level of dogmatism, prior to the marathon experience, did not appear to effect their gains in overall self-actualization.

Smith (1976) examined the obtained effect of the marathon group in a college dormitory setting on self-actualization, as compared to a control group. 16 volunteer growth-seeking college dormitory residents served as participants, and the group orientation was Gestalt. Both immediate and long-term group effects were examined. The effect of self-disclosure on change in level of self-actualization was also examined. The participants were administered the Jourard Self-Disclosure Scale. At the conclusion of the screening interview, they were divided into two groups, according to the Self-Disclosure scores. The participants were then randomly assigned to experimental and control groups so that each group had half high and half low self-disclosing subjects. Participants also completed the

POI. A two-way analysis of variance with repeated measures revealed no significant effect for experimental control groups, level of self-disclosure or repeated measure of the POI at the .05 level. A comparison of experimental and control pre-test and post-test mean scores, however, indicated a trend toward higher self-actualization for the experimental group as compared to the control group. Level of self-disclosure did not appear to influence members's self-actualization in the marathon group.

Berchard (1976) investigated the effect of Vietnam-era military services on the self-actualization of the male veteran community college student as compared to the male non-veteran community college student. The study was conducted with 21 subjects administering the POI. The data was statistically analyzed through the one-way analysis of variance method to determine if any of the variables measured by the POI produced statistically significant differences in study group mean scores. Significant differences were detected in 5 of the 12 POI variables. Low mean scores in the non-veteran group produced the statistically significant findings in 4 of these variables. Low mean scores in the veteran samples with military services inside South Vietnam produced the significant findings in the 5th POI variable. These findings did not support the general research hypothesis in that the non-veteran sample obtained generally lower S.A. scores than the veteran samples. From this we can understand that military service in the Vietnam era has apparently enhanced the Veteran's ability, in comparison with the non-veteran community college male student, to accept himself in spite of his weaknesses, to accept as normal his feeling of anger and aggression, to be more independent or inner-directed and to function more time competently.

Martin (1976) studied the relationship between the major varibales of self-concept, self-actualization and the occupational prestige aspirations of Black freshmen students pursuing higher education in the Virgin Islands. Other variables of secondary significance which were explored included age, sex, academic major, parents's education and occupation, income, educational aspirations and plans to leave the islands. In order to test the self-concept and self-actualization of the subjects, the theoretical framework and the instrumentation was taken from the Existential Study of the Integrative Level Test Series by Thorne. Statistical application used to test the hypotheses included multiple regression, correlations and t-test. Frequencies and percentages were used with other data. The findings were as follows. (1) No relationship was established between the students's self-concept and occupational prestige aspirations. (2) No relationship was established between the students's self-actualization and occupational prestige aspirations. (3) No relationship was established between the students's socio-economic status and self-concept, between socio-economic status and self-actualization or between socio-economic status and occupational prestige aspirations. (4) High self-concept and high self-actualization were not associated with high occupational aspirations. Similarly low self-concept and low self-actualization were not associated with low occupational aspirations. (5) There was a significant difference between males and females on the measure of self-concept, with males having the higher self-concept. (6) There was no significant difference between males and females on the measure of self-actualization and occupational prestige aspirations. (7) There existed a significant positive relationship between self-concept and self-actualization.

Meyer (1977) investigated the relationship between the self-actualization of teachers and the self-esteem of their students. An analysis was also made to determine if students assigned to high self-actualized teachers have higher self-esteem than students assigned to low self-actualized teachers. The subjects were 2187 students and 96 teachers. The students's self-esteem was measured with Coopersmith Self-Esteem Inventory (SEI). Teachers completed the Shostrom Personal Orientation Inventory (POI). Their scores on the self-actualizing value scale (SAV) were analyzed and teachers scoring above the mean were classified as high while those scoring below the mean were classified as low. The findings revealed that (i) there was a significant relationship between the self-esteem scores of students and the self-actualizing value of teachers in grades seven and eight; (ii) there was no significant relationship between the self-esteem scores of students in grades one through six and the self-actualizing value of their teacher; (iii) the self-esteem scores of students whose teachers were identified as having high SAV scores were significantly higher than the self-esteem scores of students whose teachers were identified as having low SAV scores in grades seven and eight; and (iv) there were no significant differences between the self-esteem scores of students whose teachers were identified as high self-actualized and the self-esteem scores of students whose teachers were identified as low self-actualized in grades one through six.

Sunderland (1978) examined the relationship between dogmatism scores, levels of self-actualization and value ranking in 127 students. The Dogmatism Scale, the POI, Value Survey and State-Trait Anxiety Inventory were administered. The primary hypotheses generated and tested were: (1) Dogmatism is a function of self-actualization; (2) Dogmatism is a function of value rankings and (3) Dogmatism is a function of levels of anxiety. It was concluded that persons with low dogmatism scores are more self-actualized and that ranking of values is positively related to levels of dogmatism and self-actualization. The study concluded that the demonstrated relationships between dogmatism, self-actualization and value rankings provide a measure of a person's relative openness to self-exploration and growth.

Smithers (1978) examined Rokeach's (1960) claim that dogmatism is a measure of general authoritarianism among a sample of 551 British university students. It was found that both high scores (radicals) and low scores (conservative) on Conservatism-Radicalism Scale scored high on Rokeach's Dogmatism Scale, although the V-shaped Curve did include more of the conservative and of the scale. It was concluded that the Dogmatism Scale can be regarded as a measure of general authoritarianism, but with some bias towards the right.

Musco (1979) made an attempt to determine the effect of Counsellor-induced conditions of present-centeredness on self-actualization in college students at Oregon State University. A determination of the level of self-actualization of clients treated by counsellors with low, medium and high levels of present-centeredness was also measured. In addition, the researcher investigated the present-centered training effects on counsellor-responses. The volunteer sample (N-28) consisted of undergraduate psychology students. The subjects were divided into two groups—treatment and control. Each subject was administered the POI prior to treatment. Analysis of the data showed no significant difference between groups (treatment/control) and low, medium and high present-centeredness on POI post/test sub-scale scores. There was a highly significant relationship between rater judgments, thus indicating inter-rater reliability and significant differences between groups (treatment/control) on the present-centered level in the counselling sessions.

The findings, in brief, suggest that there were no significant differences between levels of self-actualization in academic achievement and that the girl students have an edge over the boy students in the direction of adjustment and self-actualizing values. No significant relationships are found between the students's self-actualization and their occupational prestige aspirations. Students with low dogmatism scores are found to be more self-actualizing. Their ranking of values is positively related to levels of dogmatism and self-actualization. It was also revealed that there is a significant relationship between the self-esteem of the students and the self-actualization value of their teachers.

4. Self-Actualization and Women

The investigators have not neglected women in their self-actualization studies. Quite a few studies have been devoted to the self-actualization of women in regard to their potential for self-actualization, their social interest, their time competence and inner-directedness, and the stability of their marriages. Recently, it was established that women have as much a drive as men for self-realization that transcend the socially imposed roles of any specific culture. An interesting feature of the self-actualization studies on women is the use of the survey type research method (Lee, 1978) and the method of application of self-actualization construct to characters in novels. (Krause, 1978)

Hjelle (1975) examined the relationship between social interest, locus of control and self-actualization with 72 female undergraduates, using the Social Interest Index (SII), the Nowicki-Strickland Adult Locus of Control Scale, and the Personal Orientation Inventory. Developed social interest is the major criterion of psychological maturity in Adlerian theory; the extent to which a person achieves true self-significance depends on the degree to which his innate potentiality for "socially useful goal striving" has been realized. Self-actualization, though formulated in a somewhat different theoretical context, also represents a conception of psychological maturity. Past studies have shown internally controlled person to be more involved in social and political issues and in mastering and influencing their environment, and to have better adjusted personalities than externally controlled persons. The study cross validated the SII as an empirical measure of social interest as conceived by Adler. As was expected, these subjects evidencing high social interest showed significantly higher internal control and significantly more self-actualization than those of subjects evidencing low social interest.

Wisch (1976) investigated the effects of a special seminar on the levels of anxiety and potential for self-actualization of mature women returning to the University as undergraduates during their first semester. The investigation also examined the effect of participation or non-participation in other University-supported activities designed for mature women on levels of anxiety and potential for self-actualization. The sample was drawn from the population of mature women entering Temple University in September 1974. There were two experimental groups consisting of 10 and 6 respectively. The control group consisted of 94 women who completed the pre- and post-test instrument and did not participate in the special seminar. The control group was further divided into two sub-groups—those who participated in other University-supported activities (N-58) and those who did not (N-36). The treatment consisted of a special seminar of 12 structured 3 hour sessions that focussed a personal identity, communication, relationships, concrete management, decision-making, problem solving, sex roles and life planning. The instruments used were PIQ, MAACL and POI. Findings revealed that the experimental group showed a significantly greater decrease in anxiety than the control group as measured by the MAACL, the experimental group showed significantly greater increase in potential for self-actualization than the control group as measured by the POI, participation or non-participation in other University-supported activities designed for returning mature women did not produce significant difference in anxiety or potential for self-actualization.

Krause (1978) conducted a study of the women in Wills Cather's prairie novels with a view to revealing the art of Wills Cather more fully by seeing them from the perspective of self-actualization and of role theory. The thesis examines the theme of self-actualization in Cather's three novels—*O Pioneers*, *My Antonio* and *A Lost Lady*—with particular emphasis on the three female protagonists who are in search of fulfilment. Cather shows that rigid limitation like dependence on men, care for household and submission to husbands may make the attainment of self-actualization for women difficult, but not impossible. The study shows that Cather has given us portraits of women who seek and achieve, in varying degrees, self-actualization irrespective of their role and station. The author reveals that the theme of self-actualization pervades not only Cather's prairie novels, but it is discoverable in most of her other books.

Desmond (1979) investigated the relationship between two self-actualizing components—Time-Competence and Inner-Directedness—and the variables of vocational aspirations, career orientation and vocational maturity of adolescent girls. The subjects were 413 girls of 11th and 12th grade in a high school. The study employed the POI as a measure of self-actualizing components. The index to career choice was used in conjunction with Roe's classification of occupational levels to assess level of vocational aspirations. Significant differences were found for levels of time competence and levels of inner-directedness on vocational aspirations as well as for levels of TC and levels of I on vocational maturity. No significant differences were found for either levels of TC or levels of I on career orientation. Similarly no significant interactions were disclosed between levels of TC and levels of I in their effects upon all the three criterion variables.

Lee (1978) explored the basic hypothesis that the degree of self-actualization experienced by females does not show significant differences between those who complete high school and those who complete a bachelor's degree, and that females who experience stable marriage do not depict significant difference between those who are higher self-actualized and those who are lower self-actualized. The survey type research method was employed. The questionnaire with two instruments—the POI and the MRI—were administered to the sample subjects. The overall results of the 12 POI scales from the findings of the study showed that (1) there was no significant difference in the level of a female's self-actualization between college and high school students; (2) there were no significant differences in marital adjustment between college and high school students and (3) no significant relationships occurred between a female's self-actualization and her marital adjustment. Both college and high school students of this sample were found to be non-self-actualizers, yet having good marital adjustments.

In a very recent study, "Self-Actualization and Women," Sward (1980) has come out with a bold statement regarding woman's potential for self-actualization, exploring the images of "femininity" in Freud and Rank. He has pointed out that Freud (1933) and Rank (1941), in their sharply contrasting image of femininity, espoused two radically different concepts of self-actualization. To Freud, women were basically creatures of instinct, destined by nature to function passively as sex objects and caretakers. Rank regarded this sex model as patriarchal and reductionistic. His contention was that women as well as men have a drive for self-realization that transcends the socially imposed roles of any specific culture. The master key to Rank's thinking about both men and women is the humanistic concept of self-actualization. Rank, however, used neither Goldstein's term, "self-actualization," nor did he ever approach what Maslow would do twenty or twenty-five years later, spelling out in detail all the myriad facets of self-actualization. But Rank's commitment to the overall model of self-actualization is unmistakable. He postulated that under optimal circumstances, every human being tends to move toward self-fulfilment and can be thought of as an entity which continuously develops through self-creation. And in his opinion, the woman's potential for becoming a fulfilled, independent individual in her own right is as great as the man's.

The limited studies on self-actualization of women, thus, reveal that woman's potential for self-actualization is as great as man's. The women who evidence higher social interest show significantly more self-actualization and higher internal control. The participation of women students in other university-supported activities do not produce significant differences in anxiety or potential for self-actualization. No significant differences are found in women for either levels of time competence or levels of inner-directedness on career orientation. Also, there are no significant differences between college and high school women students in marital adjustment. Similarly, no significant relationships are reported between a woman's self-actualization and her marital adjustment.

the greater gains in self-actualization would be shown by subjects with high self-concept about their physical self.

King (1979) administered the Tennessee Self-Concept Scale to 77 male and 77 female 7th-9th graders and administered the POI to their parents to find out the relationship between parental self-actualization and children's self-concept. Scores on each sub-tests were correlated between parents and their children. The findings revealed that girls showed a stronger relationship to their parents than boys. Fathers had a greater influence on their children than mothers and the strongest sex combination was father-daughter.

Kumar and Usha (1978) studied 23 Indian managers to find out the relationship between self-actualization and organizational climate. The 23 Indian managers completed the Personal Orientation Inventory and an organizational climate (OC) questionnaire. Results suggested native relationship between OC and some self-actualization factors on the variable that aroused need achievement and positive correlations between those that aroused need affiliation.

Larson (1979) investigated the relationship of frequency, range and pattern of religious experience to self-actualization. The Religious Experience Measure (REM), a paper and pencil instrument, was constructed to provide measures of R, confirming responsive, ecstatic, and revelational experiences. Validity and reliability studies yielded favourable results. In a classroom setting, 401 undergraduates were administered the personal Data Sheet, the Personal Orientation Inventory, and the REM. Results showed that high and low self-actualizers alike had religious experiences and that such experiences could not inherently be viewed as either symptoms of pathology or evidence of positive mental health. However, frequency, range and pattern were dimensional aspects of religious experience that were differently related to self-actualization.

Lucas and Taugimoto (1978) wanted to investigate the relationship between self-actualization and moral judgment. They administered the Personal Orientation Inventory and the Defining Issue Test (DIT). The results indicated, to both facets, self-actualization correlated weekly (.24) but significantly with DIT scores.

Wilkins and Krause (1977) argued that high self-actualizing subjects should have lower level of manifest anxiety than low self-actualizing subjects. The present experiment evaluated the relationship of actualization to state and trait anxiety. 31 college students were administered the Personal Orientation Inventory, the Taylor Manifest Anxiety Scale and the IPAT measures of State Trait anxiety. Results supported the Wilkins reformulation by demonstrating that high self-actualization subjects had lower trait anxiety scores and high self-actualizing subjects were susceptible to state anxiety within the limits established by their trait anxiety level.

Shorkey and Reyes (1978) examined the relationship between self-actualization and rational thinking, using the scores of 79 college sophomores on both the Personal Orientation Inventory and the Rational Behaviour Inventory. The hypothesis, that significant correlations would be found between the rational behaviour test scores and the scale related to self-actualization, was supported by 13 of the 14 correlations obtained.

Murphy, Dauw, Horton and Fredian (1976) tested the hypothesis that creativity and self-actualization are positively related. 51 undergraduates, 53 undergraduates seminary students, 38 graduate business students, and 35 seminary graduate students completed the Torrance Test of Creative Thinking and the Similes Preference Inventory to measure creativity and the Personal Orientation Inventory to measure self-actualization. Results did not support the hypothesis. The undergraduate seminary students were significantly higher than the University undergraduates in creativity and the seminary graduate students were significantly more creative than were the business students. The University undergraduates were significantly higher in self-actualization than were the undergraduate seminary students, but the business students and the seminary graduate students did not differ significantly in self-actualization.

Roco (1976) studied the relationship between the need for self-actualization as a trait of creative motivation and the kinds of preference relations (attractions and repulsions) within research terms. A questionnaire on creative motivation and a test of choices and sociometric perceptions were administered to 2 teams of researches (10 each), one with high and one with low creativity. For both groups the index of expressed sympathy was higher than that of expressed antipathy. Both the index of received sympathy (degree of acceptance by the group) and that of perceived sympathy (degree to which an individual perceives others's sympathy for him) were significantly higher in the high creative group than in the low creativity one. Only in the high creative group was the need of self-actualization significantly correlated with the degree to which the work team was satisfying this need. An individual's professional prestige was significantly related to the group's sympathy of him, to the level of his need of self-actualization, and to the conditions favourable for achieving it. The psychological factors that favour self-actualization are (a) strong integration in the work team, (b) balanced affective relation with the team and the (c) stable interpersonal relations.

Sussy (1978) studied 25 residents aged 69-93 years in 2 Israeli homes for the elderly to see if there was a correlation between the creative attitude (self-actualizing personality) and the way of coping with the process of aging and attitude towards death. Result of the questionnaire study showed that the more creative-actualizing a personality, the better is the coping with aging phenomena and the less denial of death.

The literature on what Maslow (1962) termed "peak experience" or as he put it "the most wonderful experience or experiences of your life, the happiest moments, ecstatic moments, moments of rapture" is curiously lopsided. Numerous claims have been made about the nature of those experiences and about their consequences. Most of these claims are derived, however, from volunteered accounts or from clinical studies. Little effort has been made to test these claims on broader, predefined samples of the general population. As a result, it is possible to find frequent contradictions in the literature. There are conflicting claims about how rare or how common peak experiences are, about whether they are more common among self-actualizing or disturbed personalities, and about whether these experiences produce socially significant or only personal consequences.

Wuthnow (1978) presented some exploratory findings regarding peak experiences from a systematic random sample of 1000 persons in the San-Francisco-Oakland area. Evidence is presented on the incidence of peak experience of several different kinds, on the kinds of life-style which tend to be associated with peak experiences and on some of the social implications which these experiences have. The sample was drawn in such a way as to represent youth, 16 through 30 years. The data indicated that most people had some kind of peak experiences, but some people seemed clearly to be more oriented toward "peaking" than others. Peakers tended more often than non-peakers to say that their lives were very meaningful and that they knew the purpose of life. They also scored higher on self-related adjectives concerning personal talents and capabilities. In other words, the data seemed consistent with the suggestion that peaking may be associated with self-actualization. The data also lends support to some of Maslow's assertions about the possible effects of peak experience on values. In particular, peakers are less likely than non-peakers to say that they value material possessions, high pay, job security, being famous and having a lot of friends. They are more likely to say that they value working for social changes, helping to solve social problems and helping people in need. These differences did not seem to be attributable merely to other differences between peakers and non-peakers such as differences in education, age, employment and sex.

In recent years, humanistic psychologists have begun to exert a powerful transforming effect on our culture through the study and application of various psycho-spiritual traditions such as Yoga, Christian martyrdom, Taois, Native American Shamanism, Kabbalah which is the esoteric mystical offshoot of Judaism (Hoffman, 1980) and inner consciousness. Such traditions have been found to be veritable storehouse of knowledge about area including the mind-body relationship, altered states of consciousness and individual mental health.

To mention a few instances of such studies, Kuppuswamy (1976) discussed the concept of self-actualization as developed by Allport, Jung, Rogers and Maslow in relation to the "Yoga suthras" of Patanjali. Patanjali's yoga discipline is seen by the author as a method to attain self-actualization insofar as it refers to a state of personality development in which an individual's unique potentialities are brought to full expression.

Hamon (1977), in his article "Beyond Self-Actualization," has made a significant suggestion, based on material from the Book of Acts in the New Testament, that in the circumstances surrounding his death, Stephen demonstrates development that is beyond self-actualization in scope as conceived by Maslow (1962). Hamon also presents the need for more exploration of martyrdom as a psychological legacy.

Roberts (1979) has supported the establishment of a new counselling subspeciality that will focus on the development of inner consciousness. According to him, the goal of the consciousness counsellor is to assist clients in achieving a "transpersonal actualization" above and beyond the traditional self-actualization as propounded by Goldstein, Rogers and Maslow. Particular emphasis is placed on the exploration of time, space, identity and parapsychological phenomena. To meet these objectives, counsellor education programmes need to equip practitioners with skills in meditation, relaxation, hypnosis and biofeedback.

C. An Appraisal

During the last four decades (1940-1980), a good deal of interest has been evinced by psychologists in self-actualization theory and research. All the same, one may feel that the fecundity of empirical work is not matched by the profundity of theoretical frame. This may appear to be all the more glaring, especially in view of the tremendous range of available methods and the unprecedented variety of unconventional tools at the disposal of humanistic psychologists to explore the layers of self-actualization theory in depth. Yet, this is not altogether surprising, if we keep in mind the complex and unique nature of self-actualization theory especially as enunciated by Maslow.

Maddi and Costa (1972, p. 165) point out that relatively little actual research has been directed towards testing the theories of Maslow and other humanistic psychologists. We may say that this is partly due to the fact that these theories tend to be short on operational definitions of their concepts. Humanistic psychologists like Maslow appear to be more enterprising than most other psychologists. They do embrace complex concepts which are necessary for understanding human personality. They do explore intangible matters such as the meaning of life, transcendence, and peak experiences. They voluntarily enmesh themselves in the web of ongoing real life and devise concepts as needed by their experience in such encounters.

Small wonder, therefore, if the definitions of their concepts are not explicitly tied to clearly observable indicators. Particularly complex concepts such as self-actualization and transcendence do not readily yield to the experimenters's demand for precision of description and susceptibility to measurement. Hence the need for further work in order to make their concepts more operational. The concept of self-actualization, as has already been made clear, is not a matter of one great moment, but a matter of degree and of frequency rather than an "all-or-none affair," thereby making it more amenable to available research procedures. Therefore, there is always scope for redefining the concept, sharpening the tools and techniques and redesigning the experiments in the light of empirical evidence.

Levels of Self-Actualization

The present investigation is an attempt to study the levels of self-actualization among post-graduate students. Self-actualization, as used in this study is a phenomenological construct. It is conceived of as a dynamic characteristic or aspect of the self-concept. The meaning of self-actualization as experience or action, which is in deep accord with the self or which carries forward its project, depends entirely on what we assume about the self. Two radically contrasting versions of the self are current with many variants.

One version can be identified with the Socratic dictum—"the unexamined life is not worth living." Selfhood from this perspective inheres in the uniquely human gift of reflexive self-awareness. Actions "actualize" the self when they are done reflectively and responsively to correspond to the value priorities that comprise the core of the person's self-accepted identity. Self-actualization can be said to be the cumulative product of such actions, and is accompanied by self-understanding.

A quite contrary version of the self can be identified with Jung who has elaborated it most vividly—an "iceberg" conception according to which the true essential self, the source of creativity, authenticity and value, lies mostly outside of awareness. From this perspective, self-actualizing experience erupts for the prepared person if he is properly receptive to it as in "peak experience." Thus, the term, self-actualization, can be employed to designate empirical phenomena and ethical prescriptions that are diametrically opposed. The growth movement in humanistic psychology, especially as conceived by Maslow, seems heavily committed to the iceberg version of the self.

These contrasting interpretations of selfhood may be understood in terms of Apollonian (orderly) and Dionysian (impulsive) version of self-actualization. As Maslow (1971, Appendix A) puts it, "the current Dionysian excesses of the encounter movement and the counter-culture counterbalances the massive Apollonian emphasis of our technical society."[2] The major drift of Maslow's theoretical and quasi-empirical writings about self-actualization is Dionysian rather than Apollonian. And Maslow's Dionysian bias has implications for the meaning of self-actualization.

In the present study, self-actualization is viewed as not only a life achievement and a momentary state, but also a normal process of psychological growth that occurs when a person's deficiency motives are satisfied and his defences are not mobilized by present threats. As Maslow (1971) himself points out, "self-actualization is not only an end state but also the process of actualizing one's potentialities at any time in any amount." That is to say, the human being has within himself a pressure toward spontaneous expressiveness, full individuality and identity and toward being good and creative. In other words, the human being is so constructed that he presses towards fuller and fuller being, and this means pressing towards what most people would call good values—towards serenity, kindness, courage, honesty, love, unselfishness, integration, autonomy, detachment, creativeness and uniqueness. It is the perception of qualities such as these in oneself that constitutes an individual's self-actualization.

The inducement to study this relatively complex construct came mainly from Brewster Smith's (1975) provoking critical observation on Maslow's self-actualization theory and research. In his most provocative essay, "On self-Actualization: A Transambivalent Examination of a Focal Theme in Maslow's Psychology," Smith comes to the conclusion that some of Maslow's ideas about self-actualization seem "to purvey a one-sided, though admirable, vision of human potentiality and to fall short of full justice to the distinctively human nature of the historical domain of human choice." (p. 32)

Smith has raised three important points. The first is concerned with the way Maslow selected his "sample" of self-actualizing people. Finding that Maslow selected people for whom, after close scrutiny, he had the highest admiration as human specimens, he says that Maslow's empirical definitions of psychological health or self-actualization rests, at root, on his own implicit values that underlie this global judgment.

The second point pertains to Maslow's doctrine of human potentiality which is rooted in biology. Arguing that the young person has an extremely broad range of multiple potentialities, and that vice and evils are as much in the range of human potentiality as virtue, Smith feels that "our biology cannot be made to carry our ethics as Maslow would have it." (p. 25)

The third point refers to the meaning of "peak experiences" as glimpses or criteria of self-actualization. Smith thinks that it is questionable to give as much weight to peak experience as Maslow does in a purportedly general "Psychology of Being." While granting that peak experiences in love, nature and music contribute very much to the personal richness and value of life, he does not regard the "gut feel" as more enduringly valid than the considered thought, the passively eruptive as "higher" and "truer" than the actively sought. (p. 27)

Smith's criticism of Maslow's theory of self-actualization may appear, at its face value, to be plausible. But once we remember that Maslow's theory of self-actualization is a hypothesis, we find Smith's criticism untenable. Maslow is so modest about the inadequacies and technical flaws of his study of self-actualizing people and so informal about reporting it that it seems quite unfair to criticize him in this respect. Maslow has not presented his definition of self-actualization as scientifically final, but as an insight or a hypothesis that requires checking and validation. The strength of Maslow's theory, however, lies in its ability to explain and predict behavioral phenomena. And the evidence to support Maslow's position comes from many disciplines. Anyone who examines the available evidence of a biological basis for ethical principles will find his theory of self-actualization most impressive. Furthermore, self-actualization, as conceived by Maslow, is not a matter of one great moment, but a matter of degree and frequency. Hence its amenability to available research procedures.

In view of the observation mentioned above, it was thought fruitful in the present investigation to use self-actualization as a unitary construct, to develop a tool to measure it following the standard psychometric procedures of test construction, to test hypotheses relating to self-theory and to employ some objective variables along with some phenomonological variables.

A. The Problem

The problem posed for investigation in this study is whether people with varying degrees of self-actualization will also vary in regard to their behaviour and experience. In other words, the purpose is to know whether or not a person with high degrees of self-actualization differs from a person with low degree of self-actualization with regard to certain behavoiural variables such as the desire to seek approval of others, rigidity versus flexibility in thought and action, identification of locus of control of reinforcement within oneself versus outside the self, and with regard to certain phenomenological variables such as acceptance of self as indicated by self-ideal discrepancy, acceptance of others and acceptance of the world around. An answer to the question raised involves the development of a suitable tool to measure self-actualization, identification of individuals at certain levels of self-actualization and investigation of these individuals with various measures of behaviour and experience.

B. The Hypotheses

From the problem stated above, the following hypotheses were derived:

1. People of high self-actualization are directed more by internal than external reinforcements compared with those of low self-actualization.

2. People of high self-actualization are more flexible and less rigid in their behaviour than those of low self-actualization.
3. People of high self-actualization are lower in seeking approval of others than those of low self-actualization.
4. People of high self-actualization are more capable of accepting themselves than those of low self-actualization.
5. People of high self-actualization are more capable of accepting others than those of low self-actualization.
6. People of high self-actualization are more capable of accepting the world around them than those of low self-actualization.

C. The Procedure

In order to test the above hypotheses, the investigation was planned and executed in two parts. The first part, concerning the development and standardization of an inventory to assess self-actualization, consisted of the following steps.

1. Collection and editing of the items to be included in the inventory.
2. Administration of the provisional form of the inventory to a group of 400 post-graduate students, item analysis of the data and complication of the final inventory with valid items.
3. Administration of the final form of the Self-Actualization Inventory (S-A Inventory) to a larger group of 1000 post-graduate students to estimate the reliability, to establish the norms and to study the nature of the distribution of the scores.

The second part, concerning the comparative study of samples representing the three levels of self-actualization on several variables, consisted of the following steps.

1. To draw from the normative group of 1000, three samples of 25 subjects each to represent high self-ac-

tualization group (H.S.A), moderate self-actualization group (M.S.A) and low self-actualization group (L.S.A).

2. To administer to all the 75 persons individually
   (a) Rotters's test of locus of control.
   (b) The Gough-Sanford Rigidity Scale.
   (c) Maslow-Crowne test of Approval Motive.
   (d) An Osgood type of Somantic Differential Scale describing
      (i) Self.
      (ii) Ideal Self.
      (iii) Man in General
      (iv) Ideal Man.
      (v) General Environment.
      (vi) Ideal Environment.
3. To compare the three groups on all the variables using appropriate statistical procedures.

D. The Subjects

In all, over 1400 subjects participated in this study. Among them, 400 were used for the purpose of standardization of the S-A Inventory. The other 1000 constituted the normative group. The three experimental samples of 25 persons each were drawn from this group of 1000 to test hypotheses one through six concerning the comparative study of various levels of self-actualization on the variables mentioned earlier. All the subjects studied were post-graduate students studying various courses in Sri Venkateswara University (Tirupati, Andhra Pradesh, India) and Sri Krishnadevaraya University, Anantapur (Andhra Pradesh, India). The subjects belonged to the faculties of humanities, sciences and social sciences. Their age ranged from 19 to 31. The two Universities mentioned are situated in a semi-urban area and the students who are admitted to these institutions represent a cross-section of similar population in these parts of the country. The other necessary details concerning the subjects will be provided at appropriate places.

Measurement of Self-Actualization and its Characteristics

The investigation was executed in two parts—measurement of self-actualization and investigation of some of the characteristics of self-actualization.

A. Measurement of Self-Actualization

Self-actualization as a construct has been measured mainly by the Personal Orientation Inventory (POI) developed by Shostrom (1964, 1966). The POI is a forced-choice questionnaire (two-choices per item) requiring approximately 30 minutes to complete. The inventory has twelve scales, the first two of which are scales of Personal Orientation. The remaining ten scales seek to measure conceptually independent aspects of self-actualization.

The POI consists of 150 paired items. The subject is asked to select the one of a pair that is true of himself. Responses are scored along four major scales and ten subsidiary scales. Two of the major scales define a time ratio and two a support ratio. The time ratio assesses the effective use of time in the present including a constructive use of the past and of future expectations. The support ratio defines relative autonomy by assessing a balance between other-directedness and inner-directedness. Other-directedness persons tend to be dependent, whereas inner-directed persons tend to be self-willed. A self-actualizing person transcends and integrates both orientations. And this transcendence expresses itself in an optimal ratio between other-directedness and inner-directedness. The subsidiary scales purport to tap values of self-actualization (SAV), existentially (EX) feelings reactivity (Fr), spontaneity (S), Self-regard (Sr), Self-acceptance (Se), Synergy (sy), Acceptance of Aggression (A) and the capacity for Intimate Contact (C).

Since the POI first appeared, there has been increasing evidence of its validity. These validity studies have been reviewed by Shostrom (1966) and by Fox, Knapp and Michael (1968). Most of these reports have demonstrated that the instrument does differentiate between groups of subjects nominated by clinicians as representing different categories of self-actualization and non-self-actualization. Some of the studies have presented correlations between POI scores and scores of other personality measures for normals and for patients. The POI has been employed as a criterion measure in changes towards self-actualization in sensitivity groups (Culbert, Clark and Bobels, 1968) and the relationship of self-actualization to neuroticism and extroversion (Knapp, 1965).

Braun and Asta (1969) administered the POI to three groups of under-graduates under both standard and ideal-self instruction. Contrary to earlier studies, which compared scores under standard vs. "good impression" instructions, results were consistent across the 12 scales. Thus on 6 scales, subjects consistently appeared more self-actualized under ideal-self instructions while on 4 others the reverse was true. Inner-directedness regarded by Knapp (1968) as the single most representative overall measure of self-actualization, and capacity for Intimate Contact were not affected significantly by the different instructions in any of the groups.

Mahoney and Hartenett (1973) administered the Time Competence Scale from the POI to 28 male and 47 female college students and found that self-actualizing individuals manifested greater congruence between their real and ideal self-concepts than did non-actualization persons. Dominance was seen as a significantly more desirable integrative mechanism by the non-self-actualizing subjects. There was a non-significant trend in the desirability of an increase in acceptance as a function of the degree of self-actualization.

The Q-sort technique was also used to measure the level of self-actualization by Curtis and Cundiff (1969). The major hypothesis was that consumers who have been able to obtain a high level of satisfaction of the self-actualization need will have different product perceptions from those consumers at a low level of satisfaction of the self-actualization need. The test revealed that there is no difference in product perceptions between the HSA and LSA groups in the way they perceive their self-actualization need.

Although the POI compares favourably in reliability to other personality tests (e.g. Irlardi and May, 1968; Klavetter and Mogar, 1967), it is "fakable" by subjects schooled in subjects of self-actualization. (Brown, 1966) Furthermore, it is apparently quite difficult for the average person who lacks knowledge of self-actualizing theory to represent himself favourably in that respect (Foulds and Warehime, 1971). We may conclude that while the POI in its present form is not completely satisfactory from a psychometric point of view, it does offer promise as a new instrument. However, there is a need for additional studies which employ a variety of samples.

The POI and Q-sort techniques are, no doubt, measures of self-actualization, but they pertain only to certain specified area of experience. Self-actualization, as envisaged in this study, is a generalized phenomenological construct. Naturally, it encompasses several areas of an individual's self-experience and his perceived adequacy or otherwise thereof. Moreover, the POI is an ominibus type of test, tapping several other areas of personality in addition to self-actualization. So, it was found uneconomical to administer the POI to obtain a single measure on self-actualization. Also, it was found inadvisable to select only the relevant items from the POI for the measurement of self-actualization. In view of these difficulties, it was decided to construct a new scale rather than using the POI.

Development of the S-A Inventory

1. Collection of the Items

A theoretical guideline was necessary to collect items for the inventory. For this purpose, the writings of significant self-oriented theorists—Maslow (1954, 1962), Rogers (1951, 1961), Reisman, Glazer and Denney (1950) and Brammer and Shostrom (1960) were scanned. Based on the views of these writers, in general, and those of Maslow, in particular, a self-actualizing person was conceptualized as one who accepts himself, others and Nature, who positively likes solilude and privacy, who is spontaneous in behaviour, democratic in outlook, strongly ethical, relatively autonomous in functioning, creative in expression of healthy personality, benevolent in outlook on life, and has continued freshness of appreciation, mystic experiences, profound interpersonal relations, philosophical sense of humour and resistance to enculturation.

Having these elements as a rough guide, 200 items were collected, edited and written as "I" statements. A typed form of these items was given to a group of 20 persons with a request to strike off those times which they thought were not related to self-actualization. The remaining items were scrutinized by four psychologists—two Research Assistants, the supervisor of this study and the Investigator herself—from the point of view of theoretical relevance. This resulted in the formation of an Inventory with 155 items.

2. The Provisional S-A Inventory

The inventory along with the necessary instructions was mireographed to form the provisional S-A Inventory (Appendix A). Separate answer sheets were prepared with the option to answer each item as either "true" or "false" only. This instrument was administered to a group of 400 students. The students belonged to two of the University Colleges and were studying in different classes in the faculties of Humanities, Social Sciences and Sciences. Their age distribution is given in table 1.

Table 1
Distribution of the Standardization Group according to the Age of the Subjects

Age	No. of subjects
19	2
20	13
21	92
22	109
23	88
24	47
25	19
26	14
27	8
28	5
29	2
30	—
31	1
N = 400	

3. Administration of the Inventory

All the subjects were tested during working hours. No groups in any testing session exceeded fifty subjects. All the testing was done by the investigator herself mostly in the presence of the teacher in charge of the class. The class teacher introduced the investigator to the subjects as a Research Scholar from the Department of Psychology interested in conducting some research on human personality. Then, copies of the inventory along with the answer sheets were distributed among the students. The test was essentially self-administering since all the directions needed were given on each form. However, to ensure clear understanding, the instructions were read out aloud by the investigator as the subjects followed them on the first page of the test form. Almost all the subjects evinced interest in taking the test. Usually, the inventory was completed within

50 minutes. Following the same procedure, answers were obtained from the 400 subjects.

4. Scoring

The answers were scored according to the key prepared for this purpose. All the positive items, answered positively, and the negative items, answered negatively, were given one point each. The positive items, answered negatively, and the negative items, answered positively, received a score of a zero each. The answer sheet with the scoring key is shown in Appendix B. The above procedure yielded each individual a score that was indicative of his level of self-actualization. The items were keyed in such a way that the higher the score, the higher was the level of self-actualization. The distribution of the scores and the relevant statistics are given in table 2.

Table 2
Distribution of Scroes of the Standardization Group on the Provisional S-A Inventory

Scores	No. of Individuals
50-59	2
60-69	4
70-79	99
80-89	153
90-99	92
100-109	39
110-119	9
120-129	1
130-139	1
N = 400 M = 86.825	S.D = 10.97

5. Item Analysis of the Provisional S-A Inventory

For the purpose of determining the degree to which each item was effective in discriminating between those with high and low self-actualization, an item analysis of the data obtained from the above sample was undertaken using extreme groups. Following Kelley (1939), 27 per cent of the top and 27 per cent of the bottom scorers were used as the extreme groups. That is, the scores of the top 100 subjects and those of the bottom 100 subjects were analyzed. (Only 371 out of 400 subjects were used in items analysis.) The percentage of "true" and "false" answers for each item in each group was separately determined. Then, the relationship (biserial correlation) between the score on each item and the score on the total test was determined with the help of Flanagan's table (Thorndike, 1949) of normalized biserial coefficients. According to this procedure, an item is considered good when it is correlated well with the total score in that it is measuring some portion of the same behaviour dimension. The validity coefficients for all the 155 items of the provisional inventory are presented in Appendix C.

For all research purposes, items which have validity indices of .20 or more are regarded as satisfactory. For the purpose of this study, the 70 most valid items whose validity indices ranged from .55 to .175 were selected. The items selected are indicated in Appendix C.

6. The Final S-A Inventory

The seventy items which were found to be highly discriminative of the high and low self-actualization groups constituted the final S-A Inventory. These are given in Appendix D. Since the items as scored in the provisional inventory were found to be highly discriminative, the same scoring procedure was retained for the items of the final inventory. A printed answer sheet used in the study is presented in Appendix E which also shows the scoring system.

The S-A Inventory was administered to a group of 1000 students. The students belonged to two colleges, namely (i) The University College of Science and Humanities, Tirupati and (ii) The University College of Science and Humanities, Anantapur. The age distribution of the group is given in table 3.

Table 3
Distribution of the Normative Group according to the Age of the Subjects

Age	No. of subjects
19	3
20	29
21	219
22	284
23	221
24	124
25	51
26	37
27	12
28	10
29	7
30	2
31	1
	N = 1000

Here again, the students were tested by the investigator during their working hours in the presence of their respective class teachers. The procedure adopted was the same as used in the administration of the provisional inventory. The maximum time taken to complete the inventory was 30 minutes.

The 1000 answer sheets were then scored and the distribution of the scores along with relevant statistics is given in table 4.

7. Cross Validation

As a first step after the administration of the inventory, it was thought necessary to redetermine the discriminative capacity of the 70 items used in the final inventory. For the purpose of cross validation, a fresh item analysis was conducted on a sample of 200 subjects drawn at random from the group of 1000. Here again the extreme group procedure described earlier was employed to determine the biserial correlation between each item score and the total score. The validity coefficients are presented in Appendix F. It was highly encouraging to note that 90 per cent of coefficients were very much above .20, the required value to retain the item as valid. Since very few items of doubtful validity in an inventory of 70 highly valid items could do little to change the total score pattern, the final inventory was retained as an internally consistent tool to gauge the construct used in the study.

8. Reliability

The odd-even split-half reliability was calculated using a sample of 200 drawn at random from the group of 1000. The reliability coefficient as corrected by Spearman-Brown prophesy formula was found to be .64.

9. Validity

No separate validation of the inventory was attempted apart form determining the indices of items validity reported above. It is believed, however, that the investigation as a whole will provide some evidence toward establishing construct validity of the inventory.

B. Investigation of Some of the Characteristics of Self-Actualization

The second part of the investigation consisted of the drawing of three samples, namely, High Self-Actualizing Group (HSA), Medium Self-Actualizing Group (MSA) and Low Self-Actualization Group (LSA), and of studying them intensively with respect to the variables mentioned in the statement of problems.

1. Samples

The three samples were drawn from the normative group of 1000 subjects. For the purpose of drawing the samples, the normative group was divided into three blocks taking the cutting scores at M±1 SD. Those who scored at or above M±SD (43.61+6.98) (51) constituted HSA block. Those who scored at or below M-1 SD (43.61-6.98) (37) constituted

LSA block, and those who scored in-between the two limits (38 to 50) constituted the MSA block.

From each one of these blocks 25 subjects were drawn at random using Fisher's table of Random Number to constitute the three experimental samples that were used in the investigation. These seventy-five subjects were individually tested to obtain (1) an internal-external locus of control score, (2) a rigidity score, (3) an approval motive score and (4) three semantical differential scores. A brief description of the instrument used and the procedure employed for the purpose of obtaining these measures is given below.

2. Internal-External Locus of Control Scale

The subjects's locus of control of reinforcement was measured using Rotter's (1966) I-E Scale which is given in Appendix G. The I-E Scale consists of 29 forced choice items to assess the degree to which a person attributes the events that happen to him as being within (internal) or beyond (external) his personal control and understanding. This is a concept which has developed out of social learning theory, (Rotter, 1954) and it refers to the extent to which an individual feels that he has control over the reinforcements that occur relative to his behaviour. In other words, the test gives us an indication of the degree to which an individual perceives reinforcements as emanating from his own efforts (internal) versus the degree to which he believes them to be controlled by forces outside himself—luck, chance, fate or other powerful forces (external). The I-E Scale was administered to all the 75 subjects with the following instructions:

> This is a questionnaire to find out the way in which certain important events in our society affect different people. Each item consists of a pair of alternatives lettered "a" and "b."
>
> Please select one statement of each pair (and only one) which you more strongly believe to be the case as far as you are concerned. Be sure to select the one you actually believe to be true rather than the one you think

you should choose or the one you would like to be true. This is a measure of personal belief. Obviously there are no right or wrong answers.

Please read these items carefully but do not spend too much time on any one item. Be sure to find an answer for every choice.

In some instances you may discover that you believe both statements or neither one. In such cases, be sure to select the one you more strongly believe to be true as far as you are concerned. Also try to respond to each item independently. When making a choice, do not be influenced by your previous choices. Select any one statement and make a circle around it.

The above instructions were read aloud to the subjects by the investigator. Each subject was given a separate answer sheet. The items were scored with the key given by Rotter.

3. Rigidity Scale

The instrument used for obtaining the level of rigidity-flexibility variable was the Gough-Sanford Rigidity Scale (See Appendix H) (1952) which is now included in the California Psychological Inventory, where it is labelled Fx (Flexibility). Rigidity points to difficulties in overcoming single sets or beliefs encountered in attacking, solving, or learning specific tasks or problems. As Rokeach (1960) puts it, "to the extent a person is said to be characteristically rigid, his analytic thinking should suffer. The source of his cognitive troubles should be traceable to the fact that he cannot break down or overcome beliefs when they are no longer appropriate, in order to replace with more appropriate ones. (p. 183)

The Gough-Sanford Rigidity Scale, consisting of 22 items, was administered to all the 75 subjects. The subjects were asked to read each statement carefully and decide whether the statement was true or false as personally applicable to them. Each subject was given a separate answer sheet. The items were scored in a reverse direction so that a high score denoted a rigid individual.

4. The Approval Motive

The instrument used for obtaining the level of approval motive of the subjects was the Marlowe-Crowne Social Desirability Scale which is given in Appendix I. The M-C SD scale is a 33 item true-false questionnaire assessing the degree to which individuals avoid self-criticism and depict themselves in improbably favourable terms. Social desirability is defined broadly to refer to the need of subjects to obtain approval of others by responding in a culturally appropriate and acceptable manner.

The M-C SD scale was administered to all the 75 subjects. They were asked to read each statement carefully and decide whether the statement was true or false as it pertained to them personally. Separate answer sheets were provided for the purpose. The test was scored with the key given by Marlowe and Crowne themselves. (1964, pp. 23-24)

5. Self-Construct Measures

The instrument used for obtaining the three self-construct measures of the subjects was the Semantic Differential of the Osgood type (1957). The Semantic Differential used in the study is presented in Appendix J. It consists of 12 sets of bipolar adjectives which belong to the three well-known Osgood factors, namely, evaluation, potency and activity. The subject is asked to rate a concept on a number of seven point scales. The scales are defined by polar adjectives such as Good-Bad, Strong-Weak, Active-Passive etc. Thus, a subject would rate a concept such as "my self" or "my ideal self" on each of the polar adjective scales. The ratings are made in terms of the meaning of the concept to the subject. The relationship between any two sets of ratings, such as self and ideal-self rating, is determined using D-statistics.

The Semantic Differential was administered to all the 75 subjects. Each subject was provided with 6 copies of semantic differential scales. The concepts to be rated—self-ideal self; man in general-ideal man and my environment-ideal environment—were inscribed on the top of each test sheet. The instructions given to the subjects were the same as given by Osgood and others (1957). They were as follows:

The purpose of the study is to measure the meaning of certain things to various people by having them judge against a series of descriptive scales. In taking this test, please make your judgments on the basis of what these things mean to you. You are to rate the concept which is given at the top on each of these scales.

Here is how you are to use these scales:

If you feel that the concept at the top of the page is very closely related to one end of the scale, you should place your check-mark as follows:

Fair:_✓_:____:____:____:____:____:____:unfair
Fair:____:____:____:____:____:____:_✓_:unfair

If you feel that the concept is quite closely related to one or the other end of the scale (but not extremely), you should place your check-mark as follows:

Strong:____:_✓_:____:____:____:____:____:Weak

or

Strong:____:____:____:____:____:_✓_:____:Weak

If the concept seems only slightly related to one side as opposed to the other side (but is not really neutral), then you should check as follows:

Active:____:____:_✓_:____:____:____:____:Passive
Active:____:____:____:____:_✓_:____:____:Passive.

The direction toward which you check, of course, depends upon which of the two ends of the scale seems most characteristic of the things you are judging.

If you consider the concepts to be neutral on the scale, both sides of the scale being completely irrelevant, unrelated to the concept, then you should place your check-mark in the middle space.

Safe:____:____:____:_✓_:____:____:____:Dangerous

Important: (1) Place your check-mark in the middle of the spaces, not on the boundaries.

this — not this

:_✓_:____:____:____:____✓:____:____:

(2) Be sure you check every scale. Do not omit any.

(3) Never put more than one check-mark on a single scale.

> Sometimes you may feel as though you have had the same items before on the test. This will not be the case. So do not look back and forth through the items. Do not try to remember how you checked similar items earlier in the test. Make each item a separate and independent judgment. Work at fairly high speed through this test. It is your first impressions, the immediate "feelings" about the items that we want. Please do not be careless because we want your true impressions.

The above instructions were read aloud to the subjects by the investigator. When there were doubts regarding the meanings of the adjectives used in the Semantic Differential, the dictionary meanings were provided. After clearing other doubts the subjects were asked to go ahead with the task of rating the concepts. The concepts were rated in the same manner by all the subjects.

The scoring was done using the distance formula $D=d^2$ where "d" is the difference between the any two ratings of the two concepts such as self and ideal self or man in general and ideal man.

The raw data obtained with the Semantic Differential were a collection of check-marks against bipolar scales. To each of the seven positions on these scales were arbitrarily assigned the digits 1, 2, 3, 4, 5, 6 and 7 with a raw score of one for each semantic space. The D value for our purpose thus became a measure of similarity between the two concepts rated on the scales of tests. The higher the D, the lower would be the similarity between the two concepts. It follows from this that a person, who got a low value of D, perceives the two concepts such as self and ideal self as similar and vice versa. Thus, the value of "D" became an index of similarity or, to be more precise, perceived similarity between any two concepts. Since perceived similarity between self and ideal self is the main basis of self-actualization, the value of D is an index of self-actualization following the theoretical arguments put forward by self-theorists. Each of the 75 subjects was tested by the investigator individually on all the variables.

Since the testing time required for each subject to administer all the four tests was on an average 3 hours, each subject was tested in two sessions. The testing for each of the 75 subjects was completed within ten days of the commencement of the first test. The entire testing of all the 75 subjects took nine months.

Results and Discussion

The results of the investigation are presented in three sections. In the first section, the findings pertaining to the nature and distribution of the scores on the S-A Inventory are given. In the second section, the scores obtained by the subjects belonging to three levels of self-actualization, namely, High, Low and Moderate, on three personality measures are presented. In the third section, the characteristics of the three groups as revealed by three self-constructs are given. The implication of the results in relation to the problems and hypotheses are presented at the end of the chapter.

A. Results

1. The Self-Actualization Scores

The standardized S-A Inventory was administered, as reported in the fourth chapter, to a group of 1000 students from whom the three groups representing HSA, MSA and LSA were selected at random. The distribution of self-actualization scores for the group of 1000 is given in table 4. An inspection of the distribution of the scores in table 4 suggests that the scores tend towards a normal distribution which is slightly negatively skewed. This is as it should be, for most of the personality variables as measured by psychological test would normally yield a ball-shaped curve. (McNemar, 1955) The mean score for the group is 43.605, the median is 42, and the SD is 6.98.

Table 4
Distribution of Scores of the Normative Group on the Final S-A Inventory

Score	No. of Individuals
60-64	10
55-59	44
50-54	138
45-49	257
40-44	284
35-39	178
30-34	66
25-29	18
20-24	5

N = 1000 M = 43.605
SD = 6.98

As explained earlier, three groups representing the high, moderate and low levels of self-actualization were drawn from the 1000 individuals. The means, medians and standard deviation of their scores on the S-A Inventory are given in table 5.

Table 5
The Means and Medians and the Standard Deviations of Scores on S-A Inventory for the Three Experimental Groups

Groups of 25 each	Mean	Median	SD
High self-actualization Group (HSA)	54.04	53	3.34
Moderate self-actualization Group (MSA)	45	46	2.75
Low self-actualization Group (LSA)	35	35	3.16

The significance of the difference among the means of the three groups was tested using analysis of variance. The summary of analysis of variance is given in table 6.

Table 6
Summary of Analysis of Variance of the Data on S-A Inventory for the Three Groups

Source of Variation	d£	Sums of Squares	Mean Squares
Among the means	2	4535.36	2267.68
Within groups	72	718.96	9.9855
F=227.096		P .001	

The analysis yielded a very high F ratio indicating that the groups differ significantly from one another (p .001). It is but natural that they were different, since they were drawn form different strata of the distribution.

2. Self-Actualization and Some Personality Characteristics

The seventy-five subjects belonging to the three groups were tested on three personality tests and three scores were obtained for each subject. The scores obtained by each of the subjects on the three personality tests were used to evaluate the first three hypotheses. In evaluating each of the hypotheses, analysis of variance was used to study the overall significance of the means of the three groups, and further a multiple comparison of the means for the three groups was made by employing Duncan's Range Test.

In testing these and other hypotheses, it was decided to accept them if the mean differences were significant at or less than a probability of .05. In all the statistical analyses, although the data from all the three groups were used, only the data of the extreme groups were used for the purposes of supporting or rejecting the hypotheses. The mid-group was used as a reference point for comparing the two extreme groups.

As described earlier, the internal-external locus of control score was obtained by using Rotter's (1966) I-Z scale in order to know whether the behaviour of self-actualizing people is controlled by the internal or external reinforcements. The means, medians and standard deviations from the scores for the three groups selected for study are given in table 7.

Table 7
The Means, Medians and the Standard Deviations of Internal-External Scale

Groups	Mean	Median	SD
HSA	8.68	9	3.90
MSA	9.68	10	3.22
LSA	12.96	13	4.26

In evaluating the first hypothesis, analysis of variance was used to study the overall significance of the means of the three groups, and then the multiple comparison of the groups was undertaken using Duncan's Range Test. The summary of analysis of variance is given in table 8. The obtained F value of 8.23 was found to be highly significant at P=.001.

Table 8
Summary of Analysis of Variance of the I-E Scale Score for the Three Groups

Source	d£	SSS	MS
Among Means	2	250.64	125.36
Within Means	72	1095.84	15.22

F = 8.23

The difference between the highest and the lowest mean, that is, between HSA and LSA, was 4.28. The corresponding R_P Value for the three groups (r_3=2.32) obtained in Duncan's Range Test was higher than the mean difference indicating a statistically significant difference on I-E variable. The high self-actualizers scored less than the low self-actualizers on this variable. The difference between HSA and MSA is 1.0. This is lower than the R_P value for the two groups (r_2=2.2). The obtained R_P value for the two groups is 2.2. Hence there was no significant difference between the two groups. Similarly the mean difference between MSA and LSA was 3.20 and this is more than the obtained R_P value of 2.2. So, there appears to be a significant difference between these two groups. The means and the corresponding mean differences for the groups are given in table 9.

Table 9
The Means and Mean Differences for the Three Experimental Groups

Groups	Means	Mean Differences
HSA and LSA	8.68 — 12.96	4.28
HSA and MSA	8.68 — 9.68	1.00
MSA and LSA	9.68 — 12.96	3.28

So, the results indicated that the high self-actualizing subjects, as a group, scored significantly low in the internal-external locus of reinforcements test when compared with the low self-actualizing individuals. Therefore, the first hypothesis that the people of high self-actualization are directed more by internal than external reinforcements compared with those of low self-actualization is supported.

The rigidity score was obtained by using the Gough-Sanford Rigidity Scale (1952) in order to estimate the degree of rigidity or flexibility in the behaviour of the self-actualizers. The means, medians and the standard deviations of the scores for the three groups are shown in table 10.

Table 10
The Means, Medians and the Standard Deviations of Scores on Rigidity Scale for the Three Experimental Groups

Groups	Mean	Median	SD
HSA	11.80	13	4.48
MSA	13.36	13	3.57
LSA	15.04	15	2.25

In evaluating the hypothesis, the first analysis of the variance was used to study the overall significance of the means of the three groups, and further multiple comparison of the means was undertaken using the Duncan's Range Test. The summary of analysis of variance is given in Table 11. The obtained F value was 4.74 and it was found to be highly significant at P=0.05.

Table 11
Summary of Analysis of Variance of the Scores on the Rigidity Scale for the Three Groups

Source	d£	SS	MS
Among Means	2	124.987	62.4935
Within Groups	72	949.36	13.1855
F=4.74	P=.05		

The difference between the highest and the lowest means, that is, between the HSA and LSA, was 3.16. The corresponding R_P value for the three groups (r_3=2.16) obtained in Duncan's Range Test was lower indicating a significant mean difference with regard to the rigidity and flexibility dimension. The high self-actualization scored less than the low self-actualization on rigidity. The difference between HSA and MSA was 1.48. It was lower than the R_P value for the two groups (r_2=2.05) and hence there appears to be no significant difference between the two groups. Similarly the mean difference between MSA and LSA was 1.68 and even this was lower than the obtained R_P value of 2.05. Consequently, there appears to be no significant difference between these two groups. The means and the corresponding mean differences for the three groups are given in table 12.

Table 12
The Means and Mean Differences for the Three Experimental Groups

Groups	Means	Mean differences
HSA and LSA	11.88 — 15.04	3.16
HSA and MSA	11.88 — 13.36	1.48
MSA and LSA	13.36 — 15.04	1.68

So, the results indicate that the high self-actualizing subjects exhibit higher flexibility in their behaviour when compared with the low self-actualizing individuals. Consequently, the second hypothesis that people of high self-actualization are significantly more flexible in their behaviour than those who are low in self-actualization gets itself supported.

As mentioned earlier, the approval motive score was obtained by using the Marlowe-Crowne Social Desirability Scale with a view to finding out the extent to which the subjects needed social approval. The maximum score a subject would get in this test is 33. The means, medians and the standard deviations of the approval motive scores for the three groups are shown in table 13.

Table 13
The Means, Medians and the Standard Deviations of Approval Motive Scores for the Three Experimental Groups

Groups	Mean	Median	SD
HSA	20.64	21	5.6
MSA	18.96	18	4.5
LSA	16.68	17	4.3

In evaluating the third hypothesis, again analysis of variance was used to study the overall significance of the means of the three groups, and further multiple comparison of the groups was undertaken using Duncan's Range Test. The summary of analysis of variance is given in table 14. The obtained F value was 3.99 and it was significant at P .05.

Table 14
Summary of Analysis of Variance of the Approval Motive Scores for the Three Groups

Source	d£	SS	MS
Among Means	2	197.52	98.76
Within groups	72	178.16	24.80
F=3.99	P=.05		

The difference between the highest and the lowest mean, that is, between HSA and LSA, is 3.96. The corresponding R_P value for the three groups (r_3=2.96) obtained in Duncan's Range Test was 2.96. Therefore, these two groups differed significantly (P .001) with regard to their need for approval. The high self-actualizers scored higher than the low self-actualizers on this variable. The difference between MSA and HSA was 1.68. This is lower than the R_P value for two groups (r_2=2.8), and hence there appears to be no significant difference between the two groups. Similarly, the mean difference between MSA and LSA was 2.28 and even this is less than the obtained R_P value of 2.8. Consequently there appears to be no significant difference between these two groups. The means and the corresponding mean differences for the three groups are given in table 15.

Table 15
The Means and Mean Differences for
the Three Experimental Groups

Groups	Means	Mean Differences
HSA and LSA	20.64 — 16.68	3.96
HSA and MSA	20.64 — 18.96	1.68
MSA and LSA	18.96 — 16.68	2.28

Surprisingly enough, the scores are not in the expected direction. Contrary to our expectation, the MSA scored more than the LSA. Naturally, the third hypothesis that people of high self-actualization are low in seeking approval of others when compared with those of low self-actualization is not supported. The implications of this finding will be discussed later in the chapter in section B.

3. Self-Actualization and Acceptance of Self, Others and Nature

The last three hypotheses pertain to phenomenological constructs. The extent to which the subjects accept themselves, others and the physical environment they live in were investigated employing an Osgood type of Semantic Differential. The same scale was administered to all the subjects belonging to the three levels of self-actualization six times to obtain three measures.

Under the first condition, each subject was asked to rate himself and afterwards his ideal self on the same scale. Under the second condition, he was asked to rate "man in general" and later his "ideal man." Under the third condition, he was to rate his external environment as it is and later the environment he ideally wanted it to be. In each one of the three conditions, the similarity between the two concepts rated (for example, the similarity between the "self" and "ideal self," "man in general" and "ideal man" and "environment" and "ideal environment") was measured in terms of D-statistics. D-statistics provides a measure of the distance between the two concepts rated in a multi-dimensional psychological space, or simply it gives an idea of the togetherness or apartness of the two concepts rated.

The distribution of the D-statistics is not known and, therefore, a distribution-free statistics, namely, Mann-Whitney U test was employed to evaluate the date obtained from the Semantic Differential. The obtained results pertaining to the hypotheses concerning the self-concept and related variables are given in the following pages.

Our fourth hypothesis states that the high self-actualizers are more capable of accepting themselves than the low self-actualizers. Self-acceptance or self-ideal congruence was measured in terms of the D value for each subject. In this context, the higher the D value, the lower would be the self-acceptance. The D values for the self-acceptance variable for the three groups are presented in table 16.

Table 16
The D Values for the Self-Ideal Self for the Three Groups
(The scores in each group are arranged in the decreasing order)

HSA	MSA	LSA
71	60	145
35	52	60
32	42	60
32	38	52
28	36	45

28	33	44
27	28	42
26	24	40
24	21	38
22	20	37
18	19	36
15	18	36
13	18	31
13	17	30
12	16	30
12	14	29
12	14	25
10	14	24
10	14	21
9	13	20
9	13	19
6	12	19
6	11	19
4	10	16
2	9	15

The analysis of D values in terms of the Mann-Whitney U test is given in table 17.

Table 17
The Mann-Whitney U Test for D-Score on the Semantic Differential
(Self-Ideal Self)

Groups	Ranks	Score	Significant	P
HSA and LSA	834,441	3.81	Significant	.00007
HSA and MSA	712,563	1.45	Not Significant	.0788
MSA and LSA	804,471	3.23	Significant	.0007

There is a significant difference between the high self-actualizers and the low self-actualizers as well as between

MSA and LSA. However, no significant difference is found between MSA and LSA. The data indicate that the high self-actualizers have lower D values than the low self-actualizers, and the two groups fall into distinct populations that are statistically different. Thus, the data support the hypothesis that the high self-actualizers are more capable of accepting themselves than the low self-actualizers.

Our fifth hypothesis states that high self-actualizers are more capable of accepting others than low self-actualizers. Acceptance of others was measured in terms of D, that is, the rated distance between one's view of "man in general" and the "ideal man." Here again the higher the D value, the lower would be the acceptance of others. The D values for the acceptance of others for the three groups are presented in table 18.

Table 18
The D Values for the Concept Man in General and Ideal Man for the Three Groups
(The scores in each group are arranged in the decreasing order)

HSA	MSA	LSA
80	261	142
67	183	134
62	137	130
49	125	110
39	103	110
34	82	108
29	79	85
29	69	79
26	63	78
23	60	75
22	44	67
18	38	66
17	35	64
16	33	62
16	32	52

14	31	36
14	20	36
14	15	5
13	13	4
9	12	33
8	12	27
6	6	20
2	4	18
0	4	17
0	2	9

The analysis of D values in terms of the Mann-Whitney U test is given in table 19. There is a significant difference between the high self-actualizing and the low self-actualizing groups as well as between HSA and MSA. However, no significant difference is found between MSA and LSA. The data indicate that the high actualizers have lower D values than the low actualizers, and the two groups fall into distinct populations that are statistically different. The data support the hypothesis that high self-actualizers are more capable of accepting others than the low self-actualizers.

Table 19
The Mann-Whitney U Test for D Score on the Semantic Differential (Man in General-Ideal Man)

Groups	Ranks	Score	Significant	P
HSA and LSA	847,428	4.06	Significant	.00003
HSA and MSA	741,534	2.00	Significant	.0228
LSA and MSA	711,564	1.43	Not Significant	.0808

Our sixth hypothesis is that people of high self-actualization are more capable of accepting the world around them than those of the low self-actualization. Acceptance of nature was measured in terms of the discrepancy between one's rating of the environment as it is and the environment as one would ideally prefer it to be. Even here, the higher the D value, the lower would be the acceptance of nature. The D values for the acceptance of the nature for the three groups are presented in table 20.

Table 20
The D Values for the Concept My Environment and Ideal Environment for the Three Groups (The scores in each group are arranged in the decreasing order)

HSA	MSA	LSA
147	245	256
87	181	244
80	99	180
52	91	119
48	88	102
46	83	102
36	80	102
33	80	95
31	79	94
26	64	76
25	48	76
24	46	71
23	35	62
23	29	46
16	27	43
16	26	41
14	25	36
13	21	35
9	19	25
9	19	21
8	18	21
4	14	19
4	12	19
3	2	8
1	2	6

The analysis of D values in terms of the Mann-Whitney U test is given in Table 21.

Table 21
Mann-Whitney U Test for D Score on the Semantic Differential
(General Environment-Ideal Environment)

Groups	Ranks	Score	Significant	P
HSA and LSA	793,482	3.01	Significant	.0013
HSA and MSA	740.5,534.5	2.00	Significant	0228
MSA and LSA	700.5,574.5	1.22	Not Significant	.1151

There is a significant difference between the high self-actualizing and low self-actualizing groups as well as between HSA and MSA groups. However, there is no significant difference between MSA and LSA groups. The data indicate that the high self-actualizers have lower D values than the low self-actualizers, and the two groups fall into distinct population in ways that are beyond chance. The data support the hypothesis that high self-actualizers are more capable of accepting the nature or the environment than the low self-actualizers.

B. Discussion of Results

The present study was an attempt to measure self-actualization as a phenomenological construct and to investigate certain personality characteristics associated with self-actualization.

An inventory was developed to measure self-actualization and the scores of a large number of post-graduate students were examined. The scores, like the scores on most of personality variables, showed a tendency towards normal distribution.

For the purpose of investigating the characteristics associated with self-actualization, two sets of measures were used. The first set consisted of measures that could be looked upon as derived from the external or objective frame of references. These are called objective behavioral criteria. The measures used were an internal-external locus of control score, a rigidity score and an approval motive score. The second set of measures employed could be viewed as derived from the subjective or phenomenological frame of reference. The measures derived in this category were three self-construct measures—Self-Ideal Self, Man in General-Ideal Man, and Environment-Ideal Environment, obtained by using the Semantic Differential of the Osgood type (1957). While the objective tests were scored according to external criteria, the subjective variables were scored according to the subjects's internal criterion of standard.

In all, six predictions were made, out of which five were wholly supported and for the remaining one enough evidence was not forthcoming.

The first hypothesis was that the high self-actualizing individuals were directed more by internal than external reinforcement compared with the low self-actualizing people. There was sufficient evidence to retain this hypothesis.

One of the characteristics of the self-actualizing people is that they are inner-directed and self-contained. Since they are propelled by growth motivation rather than deficiency motivation, "self-actualizing people are not dependent for their main satisfactions on the real world, or other people or culture or means to ends, or in general on extrinsic satisfactions. Rather they are dependent for their own development and continued growth on their own potentialities and latent resources." (Maslow, 1954) The I.E. dimension pertains to the degree to which an individual perceives reinforcements as resulting from his own actions or sees them as stemming from such forces as luck, chance, fate or to the powerful figures in his life. Hence the relevance of using the I.E. locus of control scale to measure the degree to which self-actualizing people are inner-directed and self-contained.

Considerable research has demonstrated the utility of the I-E scale and the predictive efficiency of a measure of this generalized expectancy (Lefcourt, 1966; Rotter, 1966). The results indicate that the internals are individuals who see their own behaviour as determining their lives and what happens to them. They have been found to be more attentive to aspects of their environment which are personally relevant and the potentially useful, (Seeman and Evans, 1962) more oriented towards social action-taking behaviour, (Gore and Rotter, 1963) more involved in situations which they see as depending on their own skill rather than on chance factors, (Rotter and Mulry, 1965) and to evidence more resistance to subtle attempts to influence them. (Gotter, 1966; Gore, 1962; Strickland, 1962) Externals are characterized by opposite patterns of behaviour. Recently Bledsoe, Joseph and Baber (1978) have demonstrated that internals are more likely to be controlled, emotionally stable, conscientious, trusting, shrewd and sociable and that externals are more likely to be excitable and insecure. The results of the present study indicated that self-actualizing people, who depend on their own potentialities and latent resources rather than on other people and culture, are directed more by internal than external reinforcements.

The second hypothesis that people of high self-actualization are less rigid in their behaviour than those of low self-actualization has also been well supported by the findings of the study. Rigidity refers to resistance to change, pointing, as it does, to difficulties in overcoming beliefs encountered in solving specific problems. And rigid thinking, as Rokeach (1960) rightly observes, leads to difficulties in analytical thinking and problem-solving. A rigid person, therefore, cannot break or overcome beliefs when they are no longer appropriate.

A self-actualizing person, on the other hand, is relatively flexible and spontaneous in his behaviour, and more so in his inner life, thoughts and impulses. He "can break not only conventions but laws when the situation seems to demand it." (Maslow, 1954) However, it is important to note that his unconventionality and spontaneity are not superficial but essential or internal. That is why, for the sake of others, whose feeling he does not want to wound, the self-actualizing person at times goes "through the ceremonies and rituals of convention with a good-humoured shrug and with the best possible grace." (Maslow, 1954) But, at the same time, he "practically never allows conventions to hamper him or inhibit him from doing anything that he considers very important or basic." (Maslow, 1954) From this, it is clear that self-actualizing people are not rigid in their behaviour. Therefore, by using the Gough-Sanford Rigidity Scale, it was hoped to find out whether the subjects under study had self-actualizing characteristics like spontaneity and flexibility. The results of the present investigation indicated that the high self-actualizing subjects are less rigid and more flexible in their behaviour than the low self-actualizing people.

The third hypothesis pertaining to seeking approval of others was not supported by the findings of the present study. Recent works by Conn (1962), and Crowne and Liverant (1963) suggest that individuals with a high need for approval are more defensive and are concerned with avoiding threats to self-esteem. As Marlowe and Crowne (1964) pointed out, "because of their desire to be favourably evaluated, approval motivated subjects are likely to be more constrained in an experimental situation and to be less likely to rationalize their behaviour or to dismiss the experimental procedure as personally irrelevant." (p. 177) The approval motivated subjects are, thus, compelled to be consistent with the public image and the norms of the existing culture.

But the self-actualizing people "resist enculturation and maintain certain inner-detachment from the culture in which they are immersed." (Maslow, 1954) They are "strong enough to be independent of the good opinion of other people, or even of their affection." (Maslow, 1954) Also, they are not generally defensive and they do not normally avoid threat to self-esteem. Therefore, with the help of the

M-C SD scale, we hoped to find out whether or not the people in question have self-actualizing characteristics like resistance to enculturation and relative independence of the physical and social environment. (Maslow, 1954)

When the investigation was planned it was thought that high self-actualizers are low in their need for the approval of others. But the evidence report indicates that the high self-actualizers are significantly more approval-seeking than the low self-actualizing. This is contrary to our expectation. This may be due to several reasons. It may be an error of measurement whose exact source is not known. It may be in the tool or the subjects themselves. The subjects may be operating under certain cultural forces that make them answer the items in the socially desirable ways. The need to be pleasant, to seek the approval of others, and to behave in modern, sophisticated ways may be dominant even in some persons who have self-actualization tendencies, especially when they are in a formative stage. This could as well be the case since the subjects of the present study are post-adolescents.

In a perspective analysis, Rotter (1960) has applied the concepts of Social Learning Theory to an understanding of the testing situation, the behaviour to be predicted from tests, and to the intricate relationships among tests, the testing situation and behaviour. In Social Learning Theory, behaviour is a function of the person's goals or needs and of his expectancies that the goal or goals will be achieved or frustrated as a result of certain behaviours in a given situation. As Crowne and Marlowe (1964) observe, "motives or goals which could exert a powerful influence on test responses would include at least the following: achievements goals—needs to attain success in an academic social recognition, or competitive business situation; needs to win approval and affection from others; and dependence-needs for help, protection and succurrence."

Although the amount of work has been voluminous and the conceptualizations have been profuse, it is not yet understood why people acquiesce, dissimulate, or respond in a socially desirable manner. Many who made use of tests of this kind faced similar difficulties. Further, some unfortunate consequences follow from the strict use of the statistical deviance model in the development of social desirability scales. With items drawn from the MMPI, it is apparent that in addition to their scalability for social desirability, the items may also be characterized by other content which, in a general sense, has pathological implications. When a social desirability scale, constructed according to this procedure, is applied to a college student population, the meaning of high social desirability scores is difficult to understand.

It was thought that the high self-actualizers seek less approval of others than the low self-actualizers. The hypothesis was not supported. We may have to work out improved tools and techniques before we come to a definite conclusion about a variable that is culturally loaded. However, the evidence report indicates that the high self-actualizers are significantly more approval-seeking than the low self-actualizers. So, our third hypothesis could not be retained.

The last three hypotheses were tested against the data obtained from the Semantic Differential measures. The three hypotheses were drawn from self-actualization theory and they refer to acceptance of self, others and nature. These three concepts have been used extensively in self-theory and research. The idea that one perceives others as he perceives himself can be seen in the writing of several theorists. Following this line of thinking, Rogers postulated that when a person accepts himself, he necessarily understands and accepts others and the world around him. (Rogers, 1951) The self-actualizing people accept not only themselves at all levels but also others and nature without question, "simply because these people are inclined to accept the work of nature rather than to argue with her for not having constructed things to a different pattern." (Maslow, 1954) Most of the studies (Berger, 1952; Phillips, 1951; McIntyre, 1952; Crandall and Bellugi, 1954; Omwake,

1954; Fey, 1955; and Zuckerman, Baer and Monashin, 1956) that have investigated this special area have found a positive relationship between acceptance of self and acceptance of others.

Based on these observations, it was predicted that people of high self-actualization are more capable of accepting themselves, others and the world around them than those of low self-actualization.

The fourth hypothesis that people of high self-actualization are more capable of accepting themselves than those of low self-actualizing has been amply supported by the findings of the study. Acceptance of self is a major characteristic of self-actualizers. The common man in our society is unnecessarily guilty or ashamed of too many things, and experiences anxiety in too many situations. But it is not the case with self-actualizers. They can accept their own human nature in the stoic style with all its shortcomings. As Maslow (1954) says, "our healthy individuals find it possible to accept themselves and their own nature without chagrin or complaint or, for that matter, even without thinking about the matter very much." The hypothesis that high self-actualizing people have significantly higher self-acceptance than the low self-actualizing ones was amply supported by the data. The hypothesis was mainly supported by the measure of congruence between self and ideal self. The results were quite in line with the expectations of self-actualization theory. That the high self-actualizing people are highly self-accepting must not surprise us. Nevertheless, we found it necessary to empirically demonstrate the phenomenon. The results of the present investigation indicated that high self-actualizing persons, who are able to accept themselves at all levels, have significantly higher self-ideal self congruence than the low self-actualizing people.

The fifth hypothesis which states that the high self-acutalizers are more capable of accepting others than the low self-actualizers has also been well supported by the findings of the study. The self-actualizing people accept not only themselves but also others with all their frailties and weaknesses in an unquestioning spirit. Because "they can take the frailties and sins, weaknesses, and evils of human nature in the same unquestioning spirit with which one accepts the characteristics of nature." (Maslow, 1954) Several investigators (McIntyre, 1952; Fax, 1955 and William, 1962) have shown that the self-acceptance is positively related to acceptance of others. The hypothesis that high self-actualizing persons are more capable of accepting others than the low self-actualizing ones was well supported by the data. The hypothesis was mainly endorsed by the measure of congruence between "man in general" and "ideal man." Indirect support had also come for this hypothesis from the scores of the relationship between "self" and "ideal self." The results were in full accordance with the expectations of self-actualization theory. The results of the present investigation indicated that the high self-actualizing people, who are able to accept others in the same way in which they accept themselves, have significantly higher man in general-ideal man congruence than those of low self-actualization.

The last hypothesis that the high self-actualizing persons are more capable of accepting the world around them than the low self-actualizing people was also equally well supported by our findings. The self-actualizing persons who fundamentally accept themselves and others are also equally capable of accepting the world around them for what it is worth. They perceive reality clearly. "One does not complain about water because it is wet, or about rocks because they are hard, or about trees because they are green. As the child looks out upon the world with wide, uncritical, innocent eyes, simply noting and observing what is the case, without either arguing the matter or demanding that it be otherwise, so does the self-actualizing person look upon human nature in himself and in others." (Maslow, 1954)

The hypothesis that the high self-actualizing subjects are more capable of accepting nature than those who are low in self-actualization got adequate support from the data.

The hypothesis was mainly supported by the measure of congruence between "general environment" and "ideal environment." Indirect support had also come to this hypothesis from the scores of the relationship between "self" and "ideal self" and between "man in general" and "ideal man." The results were quite in line with the expectation of self-actualization theory. "The general formula seems to be that healthy people will feel bad about discrepancies between what is and what might very well be or ought to be." (Maslow, 1954) The results of the present investigation indicated that the high self-actualizing people, who are able to see human nature as it is and not as they prefer it to be, have significantly higher general environment-ideal environment congruence than those who are low in their level of self-actualization.

C. An Overview

In summary, what, then are the characteristics of a person who looks upon himself as belonging to a high level of self-actualization in contrast with another who perceives himself as belonging to a low level of self-actualization? Within the limits of the present investigation, it can be said that a high self-actualizing person is inner-directed and self-contained, flexible and spontaneous in his behaviour and that he is capable of accepting himself, others and the world around him without chagrin or complaint.

A person of high self-actualization is essentially inner-directed. Propelled by growth motivation rather than deficiency motivation, he depends, for his main satisfaction, not on others but on himself—his own innate potentialities and latent resources. Directed more by internal than external reinforcements, he perceives his behaviour as resulting from internal forces. He is not only inner-directed but relatively flexible and spontaneous in his behaviour and especially in his inner life, impulses and thoughts. Anything but rigid, he can break conventions and laws when the situation demands it. His unconventionality and spontaneity are, however, not superficial but essential and internal.

A person who belongs to a high level of self-actualization finds it possible to accept himself, others and the world for what they actually are. He is positively inclined to accept the work of nature rather than to argue with her. He can take the frailties, weaknesses, and evils of human nature in an unquestioning spirit. He feels bad about the discrepancies between what is and what ought to be. Naturally, there is a high degree of congruence between his concept of self and ideal self, man in general and ideal man and of general environment and ideal environment. The positive relationship between acceptance of self and acceptance of others and the world forms the core of his personality and provides the basis for the emergence of his self-actualization tendencies.

It is pertinent to note the similarity between the self-actualizing person and Rogers's "fully functioning person." They resemble each other in many respects. According to Rogers (1961), the fully functioning person is not in some static state of perfection, but in the process of becoming everything that he actually is. He is moving toward complete knowledge of himself and his full range of experience. Like the self-actualizing person, he is characterized by "internal locus of evaluation," "organismic valuing process," and by capability of "understanding and accepting others." (William and Arndt, 1974)

The self-actualizing person also resembles the adequate person portrayed by Combs and Snygg (1959). According to them, the adequate persons are characterized by positive self-perceptions, capacity for self-acceptance and capacity to perceive themselves as closely identified with others. As can be seen from the findings of the present study, the self-actualizing people reveal the first two characteristics of the adequate person.

People of low self-actualization are found to be externals rather than internals, directed more by external than internal reinforcements. They seem to depend more on outward forces like luck, chance and fate than on their own potentialities and resources. They are likely to be insecure too. They are also found to resist change. Naturally, they find it difficult to break conventions or overcome beliefs. They experience difficulty in analytical thinking and problem-solving. Again, the low self-actualizing people are found to be low in accepting themselves, others and the world. They do not have enough faith in themselves or in others. They are unable to see human nature as it is. Small wonder, therefore, if they do not reconcile themselves to what they are. They are also not fully satisfied with others nor with their environment.

A person of low self-actualization resembles more closely Combs and Snygg's inadequate persons. According to the authors, the inadequate persons are characterized by negative self-perceptions, the lack of acceptance and the inability to identify broadly with others. As seen in the present study, people of low self-actualization show a high degree of self-ideal self discrepancies which is indicative of an unsatisfactory self-organization. Butler and Haigh (1954) hold that a discrepancy between the self-concept and the concept of the desired or valued self reflects a sense of self-dissatisfaction. The low self-actualizing person, as has been indicated in the study, does not see himself as his ideal. He is dissatisfied with himself and, as a consequence, he does not accept himself. Once a person does not accept himself, it becomes difficult for him to accept others and the world. The present study also reveals how persons of low self-actualization find it difficult to accept themselves, others and nature.

An interesting feature of the present study is that the high self-actualizing people who are expected to be low in their need for approval were found to be high in seeking approval of others when compared with the low self-actualizing people. Whereas they are supposed to be strong enough to be independent of the good opinion of other people, the high self-actualizing people were found to be consistent with the public image and the norms of existing culture. This phenomenon may be due to an error of tool or measurement, or it may be due to the factor that the subjects of the present study are operating under certain cultural forces. The items drawn from the MMPI (which constitute the M-C Inventory) may be characterized by other content with pathological implication in addition to their scalability for social desirability. Also, the investigation might have been affected by the consequences that follow from the strict use of the statistical deviance model in the development of the social desirability scale. This could also be due to the fact that the subjects are post adolescents in whom the need to be pleasant, to attain social recognition and to win approval of others is still dominant. As has already been observed, it may be necessary to work out improved tools and techniques in order to arrive at a definite conclusion about such a culturally loaded variable as approval motive.

Summary and Conclusions

The aim of the present research was to investigate different levels of self-actualization among post-graduate students. The problem posed for investigation was whether people who perceived themselves as belonging to a high level of self-actualization differed significantly from those who perceived themselves as belonging to a low level of self-actualization in regard to certain personality characteristics such as internal-external locus of control of reinforcements, flexibility-rigidity, approval motive and regarding certain self-constructs such as self and ideal self, man in general and ideal man, and general environment and ideal environment. An answer to the problem involved construction and standardization of a suitable tool to measure self-actualization, identification of subjects at varying levels of self-actualization and investigation of these individuals with various measures of the personality mentioned above.

An inventory developed for the purpose of measuring self-actualization (the S-A Inventory) was standardized using traditional psychometric procedure on a group of 400 University students. The standardized S-A Inventory was later administered to a group of 1000 University students from whom three samples of 25 each were randomly drawn from various levels of scores distribution to represent high, moderate and low levels of self-actualization respectively.

All the 75 subjects belonging to the three samples were individually tested to obtain (1) a measure of internal external locus of control of reinforcements, (2) a measure of their flexibility-rigidity level, and (3) a measure of their approval motive. Further, they were given an Osgood type of Semantic Differential test individually under three instrumentional sets to obtain three measures of self-constructs—self-ideal self, man in general-ideal man, and general environment-ideal environment.

The data thus obtained were used to test six hypotheses derived from the problem concerning the characteristics of subjects with high and low levels of self-actualization. The hypotheses tested were as follows:

1. People of high self-actualization are directed more by internal than external reinforcements compared with those of low self-actualization.
2. People of high self-actualization are more flexible in their behaviour than those of low self-actualization.
3. People of high self-actualization seek approval of others far less than those of low self-actualization.
4. People of high self-actualization are more capable of accepting themselves than those of low self-actualization.
5. People of high self-actualization are more capable of accepting others than those of low self-actualization.
6. People of high self-actualization are more capable of accepting the world around them than those of low self-actualization.

The data amply supported the hypotheses 1, 2, 3, 4, 5 and 6, concerning internal-external locus of control of reinforcement, flexibility-rigidity acceptance of self, acceptance of others, and acceptance of nature, and these five hypotheses were retained.

The data pertaining to the hypothesis 3 were not in the predicted direction. The high self-actualizers scored more on this particular scale whereas they were hypothesized to score less. The low self-actualizers, who generally seek more approval of others, got less score than the high self-actualizers. Therefore, the third hypothesis concerning the approval seeking was not accepted.

Within the limits of the results obtained in the present study, the following conclusions are drawn:

1. Persons who perceive themselves as belonging to a high level of self-actualization are directed more by the internal than by the external reinforcements in comparison with those who perceive themselves as belonging to a low level of self-actualization.

2. Persons belonging to a high level of self-actualization are more flexible and less rigid in their behaviour than those belonging to a low level of self-actualization.
3. There are no significant differences between the high and low self-actualizing persons in seeking approval of others.
4. Persons belonging to a high level of self-actualization are more capable of accepting their own self with all its shortcomings and discrepancies than those belonging to a low level of self-actualization.
5. Persons belonging to a high level of self-actualization are more capable of accepting others for what they are than those belonging to a low level of self-actualization.
6. Persons belonging to a high level of self-actualization are more capable of accepting the world around as it is than those belonging to a low level of self-actualization.

Suggestions for Further Research

The study made six predictions among which five were supported by the data. The one concerning seeking approval of others, which was not supported by the data, needs to be investigated with improved tools and techniques.

The area of development and determinants of self-actualization offers challenging possibilities for further research. The following problems may be investigated fruitfully:

1. Levels of self-actualization among creative artists--actors, musicians and writers.
2. Self-actualization in the characters of great novelists like Jane Austen and dramatists like Bernard Shaw.
3. The relationships between academic achievement and self-actualization.
4. The relationship between self-actualization and leadership qualities.
5. Sex difference in self-actualization.

Appendix A

The S-A Inventory (Provisional)

Directions

The following pages contain a series of numbered statements. Those statements are true for some people and not true for others. Please read each statement carefully and decide how you personally feel or think about it, and then mark your answer on the separate answer sheet supplied.

If the statement is "True" or "Usually True" as applied to you, encircle on the answer sheet the word "True" in front of the number that agrees with the number of the item. If the statement is "False" or "Usually False" as applied to you, encircle on the answer sheet the word "False" in front of the number of the item. Whether you mark "True" or "False" please remember to give your own opinion about yourself.

This is not an intelligence test, and there are no right or wrong answers. The best answer is what you sincerely feel is true or false.

You do not have to brood over any item. Respond as quickly as possible with the first answer that spontaneously comes to your mind.

While answering on the answer sheet, please make sure that the number of the statement agrees with the corresponding number on the answer sheet.

Your answers will be used only for the research purposes and they will be kept strictly confidential. Therefore, please feel free to answer each statement honestly.

Please make it a point to answer every statement.

Kindly fill in your name and other particulars on the answer sheet in the specified place before answering the items.

1. I am able to discern the realities in life, however concealed or confused they are.

2. I can see people in their true colours and judge them correctly.
3. I cannot understand and appreciate modern art.
4. I wish there were no evils in life.
5. I can predict the future from the facts on hand at present.
6. I am frightened by the unknown.
7. I like the mysterious in life.
8. I often get into a world of fantasy to escape from the painful realities in life.
9. I can easily distinguish the concrete from the abstract as well as the genuine from the spurious.
10. I quite often indulge in day-dreaming.
11. I would be often in conflict with myself as well as with others.
12. I cannot accept human nature as it is since it is full of imperfections.
13. I think it is better to die young than to suffer old age.
14. I am guilty of my avoidable shortcomings like jealousy and loss of temper.
15. I often get disgusted with life.
16. I am completely free from pretensions in life.
17. I am not guilty of my sex-life.
18. I always enjoy my food and sleep very well.
19. I often feel sorry for what I have become in life.
20. I cannot express my thoughts and feelings quite freely and spontaneously.
21. I take every care to look better than what I am.
22. I always speak in such a way as to impress others.
23. I trust my impulse more than my thoughts.
24. I do not believe in the conventional rituals and ceremonies, but I do not mind going through them just to satisfy others.
25. I do not like to break the well-established conventions and laws even when the occasion demands it.
26. I sincerely try to reach perfection in whatever I pursue.

27. I think I possess a sixth sense which frequently guides my actions or conduct.
28. I have a mission in life outside myself.
29. I am concerned with the good of mankind in general rather than with the good of a few individuals.
30. I prefer short-term goals to long-term goals.
31. I give more importance to what I want to do than what I must do.
32. I am concerned with immediate problems, not with basic issues and eternal questions.
33. I believe in the "Sons of the Soil" theory.
34. I am genuinely and deeply interested in social service.
35. I like to spend considerable time and energy in fulfilling the tasks which are non-personal and unselfish.
36. I like solitude and privacy very much.
37. I am rather too much attached to people and things in life.
38. I cannot bear the loss of those who are very close to me.
39. I can accept misfortunes and failures in life calmly.
40. I generally lose my temper when provoked by others.
41. I am objective in my estimate of others.
42. I have considerable trust in my own wisdom.
43. However deeply I may try, I cannot concentrate fully on any thing.
44. I often get depressed by the ups and downs in life.
45. I do not mind getting things done using the influence of others.
46. I invariably count on the good opinion of others in whatever I do.
47. I am not unduly worried over the fact that others possess what I lack.
48. I take care to conform to the accepted mode of behaviour.
49. I depend upon my own inner resources for my growth and development.

50. I think that I have a right to expect due reward for the good work I do.
51. I feel that self-reliance does not pay in the present-day world.
52. I cannot fully subscribe to Keats's idea that "a thing of beauty is a joy for ever."
53. My heart leaps when I behold a rainbow in the sky.
54. As time passes, even the most interesting people and things begin to appear dull and drab to me.
55. I can derive pleasure even from the most casual and routine work.
56. I do not find the sight of sunrise or sunset always thrilling.
57. For me familiarity breeds no contempt.
58. Nothing gives me more pleasure than getting a lot of money.
59. I am capable of loving and being loved by others.
60. I regard sex and love as one and the same.
61. Sometimes I become totally unself-conscious.
62. I never experienced moments of ecstasy and bliss.
63. At times, I feel that I am at my best and at the top of my form.
64. I feel that I fully deserve all the good things that happened to me in my life.
65. At times, I feel more integrated and more at peace with myself than at other times.
66. There are moments in my life when I feel gratified in all things, as though I lacked nothing.
67. I have often felt to be at once mature and childlike.
68. I never tend to be poetic in my expression or communication.
69. Sometimes I feel that I am completely free of inhibitions, fears, doubts and controls.
70. At times I become so totally absorbed in the present that I become unaware of the past and the future.
71. I have never felt that I am a master of my own fate.
72. Sometimes I function fully and effortlessly, without strain or struggle.

73. At times I experience a sense of perfection, as though I had no deficiencies whatsoever.
74. I feel at home where I am.
75. I am usually indifferent to human suffering and misery.
76. My way of thinking, feeling and behaving often makes me an isolated person.
77. I am not always properly understood by others though greatly liked.
78. I am not at all irritated by the shortcomings of others.
79. I find it very difficult to have a feeling of sympathy and affection for all.
80. I long for a one-world government.
81. I believe that my personal relationships are deeper and more profound than those of many others.
82. I am not capable of crossing my ego boundaries.
83. I have a strong and intimate relationship with many people.
84. I have a very large circle of friends.
85. I tend to be kind to almost everyone.
86. I have an especially tender love for children.
87. I have a few admirers who tend to worship me despite my strong dislike for it.
88. I never spare the hypocritical, the pretentious and the arrogant.
89. I would rather pity than attack those who themselves are responsible for their misery.
90. I hate the idea of being hostile towards others whatever may be the provocation.
91. I am not, in the deepest possible sense, democratic in outlook.
92. I can make friendships with any one of the suitable character, irrespective of his caste, class, religion and political ideology.
93. I feel embarrassed to learn anything from those below my status and age.
94. I think I know very little in comparison with what could be known and what is known by others.

95. I can be honestly respectful and even humble before people who can teach me something I do not know.
96. I cannot treat with respect a cobbler or a coolie, however skilful and talented he is in his work.
97. I uphold the human dignity even of a scavenger.
98. I generally respect people on the basis of their status in life, and not on the basis of their individual worth.
99. I generally do things as ends in themselves rather than as a means to an end.
100. I do not find as much pleasure and satisfaction in working towards a goal as in attaining it.
101. I am quite clear and certain about my convictions.
102. I go by definite moral standards.
103. My notion of right and wrong is conventional.
104. I am orthodoxically religious though not strongly ethical.
105. I find God more in the service of the poor and needy than in an idol.
106. To me, humanism is true religion.
107. I enjoy the implicit humour rather than the explicit.
108. I value only thoughful laughter.
109. I cannot enjoy sarcastic humour.
110. I derive a lot of humour from punning, joking and witty remarks.
111. My sense of humour elicits a smile than a laughter.
112. I enjoy humour which is deliberate rather than spontaneous.
113. I do not think serious situations have a humorous dimension.
114. I cannot make a joke at my own expense.
115. I often laugh at my own shortcomings.
116. I do not mind being witty even if it wounds the feelings of others.
117. I don't think that humour has any educative value.
118. I can instinctively put common things to an uncommon purpose.
119. Whatever I do, I have a feeling that I am doing it in a conventional way.

120. Several beautiful ideas come to me naturally without much effort.
121. My experiences are often like those of a child, naive and unsophisticated.
122. I do not enjoy the unknown, the unpredictable and the puzzling events in life.
123. I cannot tolerate dichotomies and inconsistencies.
124. I can see some order even among things that appear to be disorderly.
125. I am afraid of being laughed at or being disapproved by others.
126. For me "unity in diversity" is a myth.
127. I have an urge to look at things from a new angle.
128. I may not outwardly differ from others in my dress and habits, but inwardly I differ radically.
129. I am considered strong and eccentric by those who do not know me well.
130. I follow my own norms of behaviour rather than those of the society.
131. I care more for inner autonomy than for outward acceptance of things.
132. I am a hearty extrovert liked by everyone.
133. I am susceptible to easy influence by others and their culture.
134. I cannot resist the harmful effects of my culture because of my attachment to it.
135. I am always open to new experiences.
136. My raw feeling and rational thinking go hand in hand with each other.
137. I always need recreation after any work.
138. I like the system of working hard for five days and relaxing fully for two days in a week.
139. I believe that lower needs have to be sacrificed for the sake of higher needs.
140. I feel that one has got to abandon bodily pleasure for attaining spiritual values.
141. Having long-term goals and objectives does not come in the way of my living fully in the present.

142. I get pleasure even from the pleasure of other people.
143. I experience no conflict between my basic urges and my conscience.
144. My child-like impulses do not interfere with my adult behaviour.
145. Sometimes I feel I am more than one person.
146. There is a big gulf between what I am and what I would like to be.
147. I am often torn between my self-seeking and my ideas.
148. I have never been cold-hearted or impolite in my dealings with others
149. I become ruthless and heartless at times, though unexpectedly.
150. I can very quickly recover from the death of people close to me.
151. At times, I tend to be boring and irritating.
152. In spite of myself, I wound the feelings of others at times.
153. I never become absent-minded.
154. There are instances of my having been wrongly kind to some of the most undeserving.
155. I think I am altogether free from temper-outbursts and vanity.

Appendix B

Answer Sheet with Scoring Key

Name____________________ Sex____________________
Age____________________ College ____________________
Place____________________ Date____________________

1.	*True*	False
2.	*True*	False
3.	True	*False*
4.	True	*False*
5.	*True*	False
6.	True	*False*
7.	*True*	False
8.	True	*False*
9.	*True*	False
10.	True	*False*
11.	True	*False*
12.	True	*False*
13.	True	*False*
14.	True	*False*
15.	True	*False*
16.	*True*	False
17.	*True*	False
18.	*True*	False
19.	True	*False*
20.	True	*False*
21.	True	*False*
22.	True	*False*
23.	*True*	False
24.	*True*	False
25.	True	*False*
26.	*True*	False
27.	*True*	False
28.	*True*	False
29.	*True*	False
30.	True	*False*
31.	*True*	False
32.	True	*False*
33.	True	*False*
34.	*True*	False
35.	*True*	False
36.	*True*	False
37.	True	*False*
38.	True	*False*
39.	*True*	False
40.	True	*False*
41.	*True*	False
42.	*True*	False
43.	True	*False*
44.	True	*False*
45.	True	*False*
46.	True	*False*
47.	True	*False*
48.	True	*False*
49.	*True*	False
50.	*True*	False
51.	True	*False*
52.	True	*False*
53.	*True*	False
54.	True	*False*
55.	*True*	False
56.	True	*False*

57. *True* False
58. True *False*
59. *True* False
60. True *False*
61. *True* False
62. True *False*
63. *True* False
64. *True* False
65. True *False*
66. *True* False
67. *True* False
68. True *False*
69. *True* False
70. *True* False
71. True *False*
72. *True* False
73. *True* False
74. *True* False
75. True *False*
76. True *False*
77. *True* False
78. True *False*
79. True *False*
80. *True* False
81. *True* False
82. True *False*
83. *True* False
84. True *False*
85. *True* False
86. *True* False
87. *True* False
88. *True* False
89. True *False*
90. *True* False
91. True *False*
92. *True* False
93. True *False*
94. *True* False
95. *True* False
96. True *False*
97. *True* False
98. True *False*
99. *True* False
100. True *False*
101. *True* False
102. *True* False
103. True *False*
104. True *False*
105. *True* False
106. *True* False
107. *True* False
108. *True* False
109. *True* False
110. True *False*
111. *True* False
112. True *False*
113. *True* False
114. *True* False
115. *True* False
116. True *False*
117. True *False*
118. *True* False
119. True *False*
120. *True* False
121. *True* False
122. True *False*
123. *True* False
124. *True* False
125. True *False*
126. True *False*
127. *True* False
128. *True* False
129. *True* False
130. *True* False
131. *True* False
132. True *False*

133. True *False*
134. True *False*
135. *True* False
136. *True* False
137. True *False*
138. True *False*
139. True *False*
140. True *False*
141. *True* False
142. *True* False
143. *True* False
144. *True* False
145. True *False*
146. True *False*
147. True *False*
148. *True* False
149. True *False*
150. *True* False
151. True *False*
152. *True* False
153. True *False*
154. True *False*
155. *True* False

Appendix C

Validity Coefficients for the Provisional S-A Inventory

Item No.	Validity Coefficient	Item selected	Item No.	Validity Coefficient	Item selected
1.	.195	*	28.	.18	
2.	.28	*	29.	.28	*
3.	.04		30.	.14	
4.	.2025	*	31.	.155	
5.	.16		32.	.07	
6.	.24		33.	.04	
7.	.02		34.	.235	*
8.	.06		35.	.33	*
9.	.3	*	36.	.03	
10.	.17		37.	.01	
11.	.14		38.	.21	*
12.	.3	*	39.	.12	
13.	.14		40.	.1825	
14.	.2325	*	41.	.18	
15.	.26	*	42.	.345	*
16.	.14		43.	.29	*
17.	.24	*	44.	.24	*
18.	.285	*	45.	-.05	
19.	.28	*	46.	.025	
20.	.28		47.	.00	
21.	.0		48.	-.057	
22.	.12		49.	.17	
23.	.00		50.	-.025	
24.	.145		51.	.25	*
25.	.26	*	52.	.085	
26.	.30	*	53.	.205	*
27.	.18		54.	.235	*

55.	.305	*
56.	.135	
57.	.12	
58.	.35	*
59.	.295	*
60.	.115	
61.	-.03	
62.	.29	*
63.	.24	*
64.	.155	
65.	-.12	
66.	.16	
67.	.11	
68.	.12	
69.	.13	
70.	.03	
71.	.175	
72.	.195	*
73.	.32	*
74.	.13	
75.	.335	*
76.	.22	*
77.	.085	
78.	.15	
79.	.16	
80.	.12	
81.	.02	
82.	.12	
83.	.22	*
84.	-.11	
85.	.38	*
86.	.385	*
87.	.02	
88.	.31	*
89.	.14	
90.	.26	*
91.	.29	*
92.	.45	*
93.	.42	*
94.	.19	*
95.	.335	*
96.	.21	*
97.	.28	*
98.	.32	*
99.	.10	
100.	.15	
101.	.345	*
102.	.345	*
103.	.2275	*
104.	.18	
105.	.38	*
106.	.335	*
107.	.39	*
108.	.15	
109.	.2	*
110.	.01	
111.	.09	
112.	.13	
113.	-.04	
114.	-.04	
115.	-.02	
116.	.2225	*
117.	.205	*
118.	-.075	
119.	.06	
120.	.215	*
121.	.07	
122.	.095	
123.	.12	
124.	.26	*
125.	.21	*
126.	.09	
127.	.35	*
128.	.13	
129.	.09	
130.	.19	*

131.	.275	*
132.	-.135	
133.	.31	*
134.	.2025	*
135.	.5525	*
136.	.26	*
137.	-.085	
138.	.12	
139.	-.0425	
140.	.13	
141.	.05	
142.	.46	*
143.	.18	
144.	.11	
145.	.21	*
146.	.15	
147.	.19	*
148.	.24	*
149.	.2475	*
150.	.16	
151.	.03	
152.	-.07	
153.	.01	
154.	-.075	
155.	.03	

Appendix D

The S-A Inventory (Final)

Directions

Every person has some idea of how he feels or thinks about himself. The purpose of the present work is to study how you feel or think about yourself.

The following pages contain a series of numbered statements. These statements are true for some people and not true for others. Please read each statement carefully and decide how you personally feel or think about it, and then mark your answers on the separate answer sheet supplied.

If the statement is "True" or "Usually True" as applied to you, encircle on the answer sheet the word "True" in front of the number of the item. If the statement is "False" or "Usually False" as applied to you, encircle on the answer sheet the word "False" in front of the number of the item.

Whether you mark "True" or "False," please remember to give your own opinion about yourself.

This is not an intelligence test, and there are no right or wrong answers. The best answer is what you sincerely feel true or false.

You do not have to brood over any item. Respond as quickly as possible with the first answer that spontaneously comes to your mind.

While answering on the answer sheet, please make sure that the number of the statement agrees with the corresponding number on the answer sheet.

Your answers will be used only for research purposes and will be kept strictly confidential. Therefore, please feel free to answer each statement honestly and thoughtfully.

Please make it a point to answer every statement.

Kindly fill in your name and other particulars on the answer sheet in the specified place before answering the items.

1. I can perceive the realities of life, however concealed or confused they are.
2. I cannot see people in their true colours and judge them correctly.
3. I wish there were no evil in life.
4. I am frightened by the unknown.
5. I can easily distinguish the genuine from the spurious.
6. I cannot accept human nature as it is since it is full of imperfections.
7. I am ashamed of my avoidable shortcomings like jealousy and loss of temper.
8. I often get disgusted with life.
9. I always enjoy my food and sleep very well.
10. I often feel sorry for what I have become in life.
11. I cannot express my thoughts and feelings quite freely and spontaneously.
12. I do not like to break the established conventions and laws even when the occasion demands it.
13. I sincerely try to reach perfection in whatever I pursue.
14. I have a mission in life apart from my personal interests.
15. I am concerned with the good of a few individuals rather than with the good of mankind in general.
16. I am genuinely and deeply interested in social service.
17. I do not like to spend my time and energy in fulfilling the tasks which are not personally beneficial.
18. I positively like solitude and privacy.
19. I cannot bear the loss of those who are very close to me.
20. I have considerable trust in my own wisdom.
21. However earnestly I may try, I cannot concentrate fully on any thing.
22. I often get depressed by the ups and downs in life.
23. I feel that self-reliance does not pay in the present-day world.
24. My heart leaps when I behold a rainbow in the sky.

25. As time passes, even the most interesting people and things begin to appear dull and drab to me.
26. I can derive pleasure even from the most casual and routine work.
27. Nothing gives me more pleasure than getting a lot of money.
28. I am capable of loving and being loved by others.
29. I never experienced moments of ecstasy and bliss.
30. At times, I feel that I am at my best and in top form.
31. Sometimes I function fully and effortlessly without strain or struggle.
32. At times, I experience a sense of perfection as though I had no deficiencies whatsoever.
33. I am usually indifferent to human suffering and misery.
34. My way of thinking, feeling and behaving often makes me an isolated person.
35. I have strong and intimate friendships with many people.
36. I tend to be kind to almost everyone.
37. I have an especially tender love for children.
38. I never spare the hypocritical, the pretentious and the arrogant.
39. I hate the idea of being hostile towards others whatever may be the provocation.
40. I am not, in the deepest possible sense, democratic in outlook.
41. I can make friendships with anyone of suitable character, irrespective of his/her caste, class and religion.
42. I feel embarrassed to learn anything from those below my status and age.
43. I think I know very little in comparison with what I am capable of knowing and what others know.
44. I can be honestly respectful and even humble before people who can teach me something I do not know.
45. I uphold the human dignity of even a scavenger.
46. I cannot treat with respect a cobbler or a coolie, however skilful and talented he is in his work.

47. I generally respect people on the basis of their status in life, and not on the basis of their individual worth.
48. I am quite clear and certain about my convictions.
49. I go by definite moral standards.
50. My notion of right and wrong is conventional.
51. I believe that humanism is true religion.
52. I enjoy implicit humour rather than the explicit.
53. I enjoy sarcastic humour very much.
54. I do not mind being witty even if it wounds the feelings of others.
55. I do not think that humour has any educative value.
56. Several beautiful ideas come to me naturally without much effort.
57. I can see some order even among things that appear to be disorderly.
58. I am afraid of being laughed at or disapproved of by others.
59. I have an urge to look at things from a new angle.
60. I follow my own norms of behaviour rather than those of society.
61. I care more for inner autonomy than for outward acceptance of things.
62. I am susceptible to easy influence by others and their culture.
63. I cannot resist the harmful effects of my culture because of my attachment to it.
64. I am always open to new experiences.
65. My raw feeling and rational thinking do not go hand in hand with each other.
66. I get pleasure even from the happiness of other people.
67. Sometimes I feel I am more than one person.
68. I am often torn between my self-seeking and my ideals.
69. I never become absent-minded.
70. I become ruthless and heartless at times, though unexpectedly.

Appendix E

Answer Sheet with Scoring Key

Name____________________ Sex____________________
Age____________________ Class____________________
College____________________ Place____________________

1. *True* False
2. True *False*
3. True *False*
4. True *False*
5. *True* False
6. True *False*
7. True *False*
8. True *False*
9. *True* False
10. True *False*
11. True *False*
12. True *False*
13. *True* False
14. *True* False
15. True *False*
16. *True* False
17. True *False*
18. *True* False
19. True *False*
20. *True* False
21. True *False*
22. True *False*
23. True *False*
24. *True* False
25. True *False*
26. *True* False
27. True *False*
28. *True* False
29. True *False*
30. *True* False
31. *True* False
32. *True* False
33. True *False*
34. *True* False
35. True *False*
36. *True* False
37. *True* False
38. *True* False
39. *True* False
40. True *False*
41. *True* False
42. True *False*
43. *True* False
44. *True* False
45. *True* False
46. True *False*
47. True *False*
48. *True* False
49. *True* False
50. True *False*
51. *True* False
52. *True* False
53. True *False*
54. True *False*

55. True *False*
56. *True* False
57. *True* False
58. True *False*
59. *True* False
60. *True* False
61. *True* False
62. True *False*
63. True *False*
64. *True* False
65. True *False*
66. *True* False
67. True *False*
68. True *False*
69. True *False*
70. *True* False

Appendix F

Validity Coefficients (Cross Validation)

Item No.	Validity Coefficient	Item No.	Validity Coefficient
1.	.185	36.	.32
2.	.235	37.	.45
3.	-.095	38.	.24
4.	.485	39.	.4
5.	.26	40.	.4
6.	.17	41.	.38
7.	.06	42.	.29
8.	.51	43.	.0
9.	.34	44.	.45
10.	.45	45.	.47
11.	.35	46.	.39
12.	.24	47.	.46
13.	.445	48.	.29
14.	.22	49.	.25
15.	.37	50.	.055
16.	.22	51.	.45
17.	.33	52.	.4
18.	.22	53.	.23
19.	.04	54	.37
20.	.29	55.	.245
21.	.35	56.	.37
22.	.48	57.	.275
23.	.33	58.	.27
24.	.3	59.	.395
25.	.42	60.	.06
26.	.32	61.	.41
27.	.66	62.	.33
28.	.47	63.	.21
29.	.39	64.	.445
30.	.31	65.	.27
31.	.24	66.	.41
32.	.23	67.	.06
33.	.29	68	.33
34.	-.18	69.	.08
35.	-.05	70.	-.08

Appendix G

The I.E. Scale
A Measure of Personal Belief

	a.	b.
1.	Children get into trouble because their parents punish them too much.	The trouble with most children now-a-days is that their parents are too easy with them.
2.	Most of the unhappy things in people's lives are partly due to bad luck.	People's misfortunes result from the mistakes they make.
3.	One of the major reasons why we have wars is people don't take enough interest in politics.	There will be always wars, no matter how hard people try to prevent them.
4.	In the long run people get the respect they deserve in this world.	Unfortunately, an individual's worth often passes unrecognized no matter now hard he tries.
5.	The idea that teachers are unfair to students is nonsense.	Most students don't realize the extent to which their grades are influenced by accidental happenings.
6.	Without the rigth breaks one cannot be an effective leader.	Capable people who fail to become leaders have not taken advantage of their opportunities.
7.	No matter how hard you try, some people just don't like you.	People who can't get others to like them, don't understand how to get along with others.

8.a. Heredity plays the major role in determining one's personality.
b. It is one's experience in life which determines what they are like.

9.a. I have often found that what is going to happen will happen.
b. Trusting to fate has never turned out as well for me as making decision to take a definite course of action.

10.a. In the case of the well prepared student, there is rarely, if ever, such a thing as an unfair test.
b. Many times examination questions tend to be so unrelated to course work that studying is really useless.

11.a. Becoming a success is a matter of hard work-luck has little or nothing to do with it.
b. Getting a good job depends mainly on being in the right place at the right time.

12.a. The average citizen can have an influence in government decision.
b. This world is run by the few people in power, that there is not much the little guy can do about it.

13.a. When I make plans, I am almost certain that I can make them work.
b. It is not always wise to plan too far ahead because many things turn out to be a matter of good or bad fortune anyhow.

14.a. There are certain people who are just no good.
b. There is some good in everybody.

15.a. In my case, getting what I want has little or nothing to do with luck.
b. Many times, we might just as well decide what to do by flipping a coin.

16.a. Who gets to be the boss often depends on who was lucky enough to be in the right place first.
b. Getting people to do the right thing depends upon ability; luck has little or nothing to do with it.

17.a. As far as world affairs are concerned, most of us are the victims of forces we can neither understand nor control.
b. By taking an active part in political and social affairs, people can control world events.

18.a. Most people don't realize the extent to which their lives are controlled by accidental happenings.
b. There really is no such thing as "luck."

19.a. One should always be willing to admit mistakes.
b. It is usually best to cover up one's mistakes.

20.a. It is hard to know whether or not a person really likes you.
b. How many friends you have depends upon how nice a person you are.

21.a. In the long run, the bad things that happen to us are balanced by good ones.
b. Most misfortunes are the results of lack of ability, ignorance, laziness, or all three.

22.a. With enough effort we can wipe out political corruption.
b. It is difficult for people to have much control over things politicians do in office.

23.a. Sometimes I can't understand how teachers arrive at the marks they give.
b. There is a direct connection between how hard I study and the marks I get.

24.a. A good leader expects people to decide for themselves what they should do.
b. A good leader makes it clear for everybody what their jobs are.

25.a. Many times I feel that I have little influence over the thing that happens to me.
b. It is impossible for me to believe that chance or luck plays an important role in my life.

26.a. People are lonely because they don't try to be friendly.
b. There is not much use in trying too hard to please people; if they like you, they like you.

27.a. There is too much emphasis on athletics in high school.
b. Team sports are an excellent way to build character.

28.a What happens to me is my own doing.
b. Sometimes I feel that I don't have enough control over the direction my life is taking.

29.a. Most of the time I can't understand why politicians behave the way they do.
b. In the long run the people are responsible for bad movement on a national as well as on a local level.

Appendix H

The Gough-Sanford Rigidity Scale

1. I am often the last one to give up trying to do a thing.
2. There is usually only one best way to solve most problems.
3. I prefer work that requires a great deal of attention to detail.
4. I often become so wrapped up in something I am doing that I find it difficult to turn my attention to other matters.
5. I dislike to change my plans in the midst of an undertaking.
6. I never miss going to Church/Temple/Mosque.
7. I usually maintain my own opinion even though many other people have a different point of view.
8. I find it easy to stick to a certain schedule, once I have started it.
9. I do not enjoy having to adapt myself to new and unusual situations.
10. I prefer to stop and think before I act even on trifling matters.
11. I try to follow a programme of life based on duty.
12. I usually find that my own way of attacking a problem is best, even though it doesn't always seem to work in the beginning.
13. I am a methodical person in whatever I do.
14. I think it is usually wise to do things in a conventional way.
15. I always finish tasks I start, even if they are not very important.
16. I often find myself thinking of the same tunes or phrases for days at a time.
17. I have a work and study schedule which I follow carefully.

18. I usually check more than once to be sure that I have locked a door, put out the light, or something of the sort.
19. I have never done anything dangerous for the thrill of it.
20. I believe that promptness is a very important personality characteristic.
21. I am always careful about my manner of dress.
22. I always put on and take off my clothes in the same order.

Appendix I

The Marlowe-Crowne Social-Desirability Scale Personal Reaction Inventory

1. Before voting I thoroughly investigate the qualifications of all the candidates.
2. I never hesitate to go out of my way to help someone in trouble.
3. It is sometimes hard for me to go on with my work if I am not encouraged.
4. I have never intensely disliked anyone.
5. On occasions I have had doubts about my ability to succeed in life.
6. I sometimes feel resentful when I don't get my way.
7. I am always careful about my manner of dress.
8. My table manners at home are as good as when I eat out in a restaurant.
9. If I could get into a movie without paying and be sure I was not seen, I would probably do it.
10. On a few occasions, I have given up doing something because I thought too little of my ability.
11. I like to gossip at times.
12. There have been times when I felt like rebelling against people in authority even though I know they were right.
13. No matter who I'm talking to, I'm always a good listener.
14. I can remember "playing sick" to get out of something.
15. There had been occasions when I took advantage of someone.
16. I'm always willing to admit it when I make a mistake.
17. I always try to practise what I preach.
18. I don't find it particularly difficult to get along with loud-mouthed, obnoxious people.
19. I sometimes try to get even, rather than forgive and forget.

20. When I don't know something, I don't at all mind admitting it.
21. I am always courteous, even to people who are disagreeable.
22. At times I have really insisted on having things my own way.
23. There have been occasions, when I felt like smashing things.
24. I would never think of letting someone else be punished for my wrong doings.
25. I never resent being asked to return a favour.
26. I have never been irked when people expressed ideas very different from my own.
27. I never make a long trip without checking the safety of the vehicle in which I am travelling.
28. There have been times when I was quite jealous of the good fortune of others.
29. I have almost never felt the urge to tell someone off.
30. I am sometimes irritated by people who ask favours of me.
31. I have never felt that I was punished without cause.
32. I sometimes think when people have a misfortune they only got what they deserved.
33. I have never deliberately said something that hurt someone's feelings.

Appendix J

The Semantic Differential

Instructions

"The purpose of the study is to measure the meaning of certain things to various people by having them judge against a series of descriptive scales. In taking this test, please make your judgment on the basis of what these things mean to you. You are to rate the concept which is given at the top of each of these scales.

Here is how you are to use these scales:

If you feel that the concept at the top of the page is very closely related to one end of the scale, you should place your check-mark as follows:

Fair:__✓__:_____:_____:_____:_____:_____:unfair

or

Fair:_____:_____:_____:_____:_____:__✓__:unfair

If you feel that the concept is quite closely related to one or the other end of the scale (but not extremely), you should place your check-mark as follows:

Strong:_____:__✓__:_____:_____:_____:_____:Weak

or

Strong:_____:_____:_____:_____:__✓__:_____:Weak

If the concept seems only slightly related to one side as opposed to the other side (but is not really neutral), then you should check as follows:

Active:_____:_____:__✓__:_____:_____:_____:Passive

or

Active:_____:_____:_____:__✓__:_____:_____:Passive

The direction towards which you check, of course, depends upon which of the two ends of the scale seems most characteristic of the things you are judging.

If you consider the concept to be neutral on the scale, both sides of the scale are completely irrelevant, unrelated to the concept, then you should place your check-mark in the middle space.

safe:____:____:_✓_:____:____:____:dangerous.

Important: (1) Place your check-marks on the middle of the spaces, not on the boundaries:

this ... not this

:____:_✓_:____:____✓:____:____:

(2) Be sure you check every scale. Do not omit any.

(3) Never put more than one check-mark on a single scale.

Sometimes you may feel as though you have had the same item before on the test. This will not be the case, so do not look back and forth through the items. Do not try to remember how you checked similar items earlier in the test. Make each item a separate and independent judgment. Work at fairly high speed through the test. It is your first impressions, the immediate "feelings" about the items that we want. Please do not be careless because we want your true "impressions."

Bibliography

Achenbach, T., and Zigler, E. "Social Competence and Self-Image Disparity in Psychiatric and Non-Psychiatric Patients." *Journal of Abnormal and Social Psychology*, 1963, 67, pp. 197-205.

Adler, A. *Understanding Human Nature.* New York: Greenberg, 1927.

Allport, G.W. *The Individual and His Religion*. New York: Macmillan, 1950.

------. *Becoming: Basic Consideration for a Psychology of Personality,* New Haven: Yale University Press, 1955.

------. *Pattern and Growth in Personality*, New York: Holt, 1961.

Angyal, A. *Foundations for a Science of Personality.* Commonwealth Fund, 1941.

Antsyferova, L.I. "The Psychology of the Self-Actualizing Individuals in the Works of Abraham Maslow." *Voprosy Paikhologii*, 1973, 9, pp 172-80.

Aron, A. "Maslow's Other Child." *Journal of Humanistic Psychology*, 1977, 17, pp. 9-24.

Baber, W. *The Knowledge of Man*. New York: Harper Torchbooks, 1965.

Berger, E. "The Relationships Between Expressed Acceptance of the Self and Expressed Acceptance of Others." *Journal of Abnormal and Social Psychology,* 1952, 47, pp. 778-82.

Bertalanffy, L. "On the Definition of the Symbol." In J.R. Royce, ed., *Psychology and the Symbol*. New York: Random House, 1965.

Bledsoe, J.C., and Baber, W.C. "Personality Correlations of Locus of Control Among College Women." *Psychology Reports,* 1978, 43, pp. 1129-30.

Braun, J.R., and Asta, P. "A Comparison of 'Real' Vs 'Ideal' Self with a Self-Actualization Inventory." *Journal of Psychology,* 1969, 72, pp. 159-64.

Brown, D.H., Engin, A.W., and Wallbrown, F.H. "Locus of Control and Reading Attitude." *Psychology in the Schools*, 1979, 16, pp. 336-38.

Buber, M. *I and Thou*. New York: Charles Scribner's Sons, 1958.

Bugental, J.F.T. *The Search for Authenticity*. New York: Holt, Rinehart and Winston, 1965.

-----. "Humanistic Psychology and the Clinician." In L.E. Abt and B.F. Reiss, eds., *Progress in Clinical Psychology*. New York: Cvune and Stratton, 1966, 7, pp. 223-39.

Buhler, C. "Theoretical Observations about Life's Basic Tendencies." *American Journal of Psychology,* 1959, 13, pp. 561-81.

-----. "Genetic Aspects of the Self." *Annals of the N.Y. Academy of Science*, 1962, 96, pp. 730-64.

-----, and Massari, K.F., eds. *Humanism and the Course of Life: Studies in Goal-Determination*. New York: Springer, 1967.

Buss, A.R. "Humanistic Psychology as Liberal Ideology: The Socio-Historical Roots of Maslow's Theory of Self-Actualization." *Journal of Human Psychology*, 1979, 19, pp. 43-56.

Butler, J.M., and Haigh, G.V. "Changes in the Relations between Self-Concepts and Ideal Concepts, Consequent upon Client-Centered Counselling." In C.R. Rogers and F.R. Dymond, eds., *Psychotherapy and Personality Change*. Chicago: University of Chicago Press, 1954, pp. 55-75.

Cantril, H. *The "Why" of Man's Experience.* Macmillan, 1950.

Cohen, J. *Humanistic Psychology*. New York: Collier, 1962.

Combs, A.W., and Snygg, D. *Individual Behavior*. New York: Harper, 1959.

Conn, L. "The Effects of the Approval Motive, Generalized Expectancy, and the Threat to Self-Esteem upon the Identification of Emotional Communication." Doctoral Dissertation, Ohio State University, Ann Arbor, Mich.: University of Microfilms, 1965, No. 65-7375.

Crowne, D.P., and Liverant, S. "Conformity under Varying Conditions of Personal Commitment." *Journal of Abnormal and Social Psychology,* 1963, 66, pp. 547-55.

Crandall, V.J. and Bellugi, U. "Some Relationships of Inter-personal and Intra-personal Concept Validation to Personal Social Adjustment." *Journal of Personality*, 1954, 23, pp. 224-32.

Crowne, D.P., and Marlowe, D.A. "A New Scale of Social Desirability Independent of Psychopathology." *Journal of Counselling Psychology*, 1960, 24, pp. 349-54.

------. *The Approval Motive*. New York: Wiley, 1964.

Curtis, B., and Cundiff, E.W. "Self-Actualization and Product Perception." *Journal of Marketing Research*, 1969, 6, pp. 470-72.

Culbert, S., Clark, J., and Bobels, H. "Measures of Change Towards Self-Actualization in Two Sensitivity Training Groups." *Journal of Counseling Psychology*, 1968, 15, pp. 53-57.

Deikman, A.J. "Phenonothiazines and the Therapist's Fear of Identification." *Journal of Humanistic Psychology,* 1971, 11, pp. 196-200.

Erickson, E.H. *Identity and the Life Cycle.* New York: International University Press, 1959.

Eugene, W.H. "Maslow's Hierarchy of Needs." *Journal of Humanistic Psychology*, 1981, 21, pp. 69-74.

Fey, W.F. "Acceptance by Others and Its Relation to Acceptance of Self and Others: A Revaluation." *Journal of Abnormal and Social Psychology*, 1955, 50, pp. 274-76.

Forest, J.J., and Siez, G. "Pseudo Self-Actualization." *Journal of Humanistic Psychology,* 1981, 1.

Foulds, M.L., and Warehime, R.G. "Effects of a 'Fake' Good Response Set on a Measure of Self-Actualization." *Journal of Counseling Psychology,* 1971, 18, pp. 279-80.

Fox, J., Knapp, R.R., and Michael, N.B., "Assessment of Self-Actualization of Psychiatric Patients: Validity of POI." *Education Psychology*, 1968, 28, pp. 565-69.

Frank, J.D. *Persuasion and Healing.* Baltimore: Johns Hopkins Press, 1961.

Freud, S. *Beyond the Pleasure Principle.* London: International Psychoanalytic Press, 1922.

-----. *Introductory Lectures on Psychoanalysis*. New York: Norton, 1933.

-----. *The Ego and the Id.* London: Hogarth, 1935.

Frick, W.B. "Conceptual Foundations of Self-Actualization: A Contribution to Motivation Theory." *Journal of Humanistic Psychology,* 1982, 22, pp. 33-52.

Friedman, M *The Hidden Human Image*. New York: Delacorate, 1974.

-----. "Aiming at the Self: The Paradox of Encounter and the Human Potential Movement." *Journal of Humanistic Psychology*, 1976, 16, pp. 5-33.

Fromm, E. *Man for Himself*. New York: Rinehart, 1941.

-----. *The Revolution of Hope*. New York: Harper and Row, 1968.

Geller, L. "The Failure of Self-Actualization Theory: A Critique of Carl Rogers and Abraham Maslow." *Journal of Humanistic Psychology,* 1982, 22, pp. 56-73.

Getter, H.A. "A Personality Determinant of Verbal Conditioning." *Journal of Personality,* 1966, 34, pp. 397-405.

Goble, F. *The Third Force: The Psychology of Abraham Maslow.* New York: Grossmen, 1970.

-----. "A Note on Self-Actualization." *Journal of Humanistic Psychology,* 1974, 14.

Goldstein, A.P. *Therapist-Patient Expectancies in Psychotherapy.* New York: Macmillan, 1962.

Goldstein, K. *The Organism.* New York American Book Co., 1939.

Gore, P.M. *Individual Difference in the Prediction of Subject Compliance to Experiment Bias.* Unpublished Doctoral Dissertation, Ohio State University, 1962.

-----, and Rotter, J.B. "A Personality Correlate of Social Section." *Journal of Personality,* 1963, 31, pp. 58-64.

Haigh, G.V. "Psychotherapy as Interpersonal Encounter." In J.F.T. Bugental, ed., *Challenges of Humanistic Psychology,* New York: McGraw-Hill, 1967.

Hall, C., and Linsey, Q. *Theories of Personality.* New York: John Wiley, 1970.

Hamon, S.A. "Beyond Self-Actualization: Comments on the Life and Death of Stephen, The Martyr." *Journal of Psychology and Theology,* 1977, S, pp. 292-99.

Harman, W.W. "Old Wine in New Wineskins." In J.F.T. Bugental.

Heisenberg, W. *Physics and Philosophy.* New York: Harper and Row, 1958.

Hilgard, E.R. "Human Motives and the Concept of the Self," *American Psychologist,* 1949, 4, pp. 374-82.

Hjelle, L.A. "Relationship of Social Interest to Internal-External Control and Self-Actualization in Young Women." *Journal of Individual Psychology,* 1975, 31, pp. 171-74

Hoffman, S., and Tosi, D.J. "A Factor Analysis of the Personal Orientation Inventory." *Journal of Humanistic Psychology*, 1980, pp. 86-92.

Irlardi, R.L., and May, W.T. "A Reliability Study of Shostrom's POI." *Journal of Humanistic Psychology*, 1968, 8, pp. 68-72.

James, W. *The Varieties of Religious Experience.* Modern Lib., 1942.

Johnson, S., and Johnson, N. "Effects of Various Groups Approaches on Self-Actualization." *Journal of Counseling Psychology*, 1979, 26, pp. 444-47.

Jung, C.G. *Modern Man in Search of a Soul*. New York: Harcourt, 1933.

Katz, P., and Zigler, E. "Self-Image Disparity: A Developmental Approach." *Journal of Personality and Social Psychology*, 1967, 5, pp. 186-95.

Kelley, G.P. "Guided Fantasy as a Counseling Technique with Youth." *Journal of Counseling Psychology*, 1972, 19, pp. 355-61.

Kilmann, P.R., Sotile, W.M. and Fritz, K.R. "Marathon Versus Weekly Encounter Group Treatment on Self-Actualization: Two Years Later." *Group and Organization Studies*, 1978, 3, pp. 483-88.

Kiss, I.A.L. "A Comparison of Self-Actualization, Adjustment and Sociometric Status of High School Students." Fordam University, 1975.

King, M. "Parental Self-Actualization and Children's Self-Concept." *Psychological Reports*, 1979, 44, pp. 80-82.

Klavatter, R.E. and Mogar, R. "Stability and Internal Consistency of a Measure of Self-Actualization." *Psychological Reports*, 1967, 21, pp. 422-24.

Knapp, R.R. "Relationship of a Measure of Self-Actualization to Neuroticism and Extraversion." *Journal of Consulting Psychology*, 1965, 29, pp. 168-72.

Koch, S. "The Image of Man Implicit in Encounter Group Theory." *Journal of Humanistic Psychology*, 1971, 11, pp. 109-28.

Krause, J.B. *Self-Actualization in Wills Cather's Prairie Novels*. The University of Nebraska, Lincoln, 1978, p. 188.

Krutch, W. *Human Nature and Human Condition*. Random House, 1959.

Kumar, U. "Self-Actualization and Organization Climate: A Study of Indian Managers." *Indian Journal of Clinical Psychology*, 1978, 5, pp. 161-66.

Kuppuswamy, B. "Yoga and Self-Actualization." *Manas*, 1976, 23, pp. 131-41.

Larsen, J.A. "Self-Actualization as Related to Frequency Range and Pattern of Religious Experience." *Journal of Psychology and Theology*, 1979, 7, pp. 31-47.

Lacky, P. *Self-Consistency: A Theory of Personality.* New York: Island Press, 1951.

Lefcourt, H.M. "Internal Versus External Control of Reinforcement: A Review." *Psychological Bulletin,* 1966, 65, pp. 206-20.

Levine, L.S. *Personal and Social Development: The Psychology of Effective Behaviour.* New York: Holt, Rinehart and Winston, 1963.

Lifton, R.J. "Psychological Effects of the Atomic Bomb in Hiroshima: The Theme of Death." *Daedalus*, 1963, 92, pp. 426-97.

Liverant, S. "Learning Theory and Clinical Psychology." In L.E. Abt and B.F. Reiss, eds., *Progress in Clinical Psychology*, Vol. 5. New York: Grune and Stratton, 1963.

Lucas, L.F., and Tsugimote, R.N. Self-Actualization and Moral Judgement." *Psychological Reports,* 1978, 43, p. 838.

Mahoney, J., and Hartenett, J. "Self-Actualization and Self-Ideal Discrepancy." *Journal of Psychology,* 1977, 5, pp. 292-99.

Maslow, A.H. "A Theory of Human Motivation." *Psychological Review,* 1943, 50, pp. 370-96.

-----. *Motivation and Personality*. New York: Harper and Row, 1954.

-----. "Comments on Dr. Old's Paper." In M.R. Jones, ed., *Enebraska Symposium on Motivation*. University of Enebraska, 1955.

-----. ed. *New Knowledge in Human Values.* New York: Harper and Row, 1959.

-----. *Toward a Psychology of Being.* Princeton, N.J.: Van Nostrand, 1962.

-----. *Religious Values and Peak Experiences.* Columbus, Ohio: Ohio State University Press, 1964.

-----. "Humanistic Science and Transcendent Experience." *Journal of Humanistic Psychology,* 1965, 5, pp. 219-27.

-----. *The Psychology of Science: A Reconnaisance.* New York: Harper and Row, 1966.

-----. "Self-Actualization and Beyond." In Bugental, *Challenges of Humanistic Psychology.*

-----. "Existential Psychology--What is in it for us?" In R. May, ed., *Existential Psychology*.

-----. "Humanistic Education Vs. Professional Education: Further Comments." *New Directions in Teaching.* Bowling Green University, 1970.

-----. *The Farther Reaches of Human Nature*. New York: Viking, 1972.

May, R., ed., *Existential Psychology*. Random House, 1961.

-----. "Intentionality: The Heart of Human Will." *Journal of Humanistic Psychology*, 1965, 5, pp. 202-9.

Meyer, M.M., ed. *The Relationship of the Self-Esteem of Students to the Self-Actualization of Teachers*. Northern Illinois University, 1977.

McIntyre, C.J. "Acceptance by Others and Its Relation to Acceptance of Self and Others." *Journal of Abnormal Psychology,* 1952, 47, pp. 624-26.

McNemar, Q. *Psychological Statistics*. New York: Wiley, 1955.

Mogar, R.E. "Psychodelic LSD Research: A Critical Review of Methods and Results." In J.F.T. Bugental, ed., *Challenges of Humanistic Psychology*.

-----. "Current Status and Future Trends in Psychedelic Research." *Journal of Humanistic Psychology,* 1965, 5, pp. 145-47.

Moustakas, C., ed. *The Self*. Harper, 1956.

Murphy, J.P., et al. "Self-Actualization and Creativity." *Journal of Creative Behaviour,* 1976, 10, pp. 39-44.

Murphy, G. *Human Potentialities*. New York: Basic Books, 1958.

Murray, H.A., et al. *The Assessment of Men*. New York: Holt, Rinchart and Winston, 1948.

Omwake, K.T. "The Relationship Between Acceptance of Self and Acceptance of Others Shown by Three Personality Inventories." *Journal of Consulting Psychology,* 1954, 18, pp. 443-46.

Ornstein, R.E. *The Psychology of Consciousness.* San Francisco: Freeman, 1972.

Osgood, C.E., Suci, G.J., and Tamnenbaum, P.H. *The Measurement of Meaning.* Urbana Illinois : University of Illinois Press, 1957.

Ott, J., and Geyer, M. "Report on Self-Actualizing Group After Sixteen Months." *Psychioctric Neusologie and Medizinische,* 1972, 24, pp. 210-15.

Peteroy, E.T. "Effect of Member and Leader Expectations on Group Outcome." *Journal of Counseling Psychology,* 1979, 26, pp. 462-65.

Phillips, E.L. "Attitude Towards Self and Others: A Brief Questionnaire Report." *Journal of Consulting Psychology,* 1951, 15, pp. 79-81.

Polanyi, M. *Personnel Knowledge.* Chicago: University of Chicago Press, 1958.

Rank, O. *Beyond Psychology.* New York: Dover, 1941.

Reddy, W.B., and Beers, T. "Sensitivity Training and the Healthy Become Self-Actualized: Small Group Behaviour." *Community Psychology,* 1977, 8, pp. 525-32.

Reisman, D. *The Lonely Crowd.* New Haven: Yale University Press, 1950.

Roberts, T.B. "Conscious Counseling: New Roles and New Goals." *Elementary School Guidance and Counseling,* 1979, 14, pp. 103-7.

Roco, M. "Motivation and Preference in Research Teams of High and Low Creativity." *Revista de Psichologie,* 1976, 22, pp. 377-93.

Rogers, C.R. *Client-Centred Therapy.* Boston: Houghton Mifflin, 1951.

-----. *On Becoming a Person.* Boston: Houghton Mifflin, 1951.

-----. "Some Thoughts Regarding the Current Philosophy of the Behavioral Sciences." *Journal of Humanistic Psychology,* 1965, 5, pp. 182-94.

Rokeach, M. *The Open and Closed Mind.* New York: Basic Books, 1960.

Rotter, J.B., Chance, J.E., and Phares, E.J. *Applications of a Social Learning Theory of Personality.* New York: Holt, Rinehart and Winston, 1972.

-----. "Generalized Expectancies for Internal Versus External Control of Reinforcement." *Psychological Monographs,* 1966, 80, (whole No. 609).

-----. *Social Learning and Clinical Psychology.* Englewood Cliffs, N.J.: Prentice-Hall, 1954.

-----, and Mulry, R.C. "Internal Versus External Control of Reinforcement and Decision Time." *Journal of Personality and Social Psychology,* 1965, 2, pp. 598-604.

-----. "Some Implications of a Social Learning Theory for the Prediction of Goal-Directed Behaviour from Testing Procedures." *Psychological Review,* 1960, 67, pp. 201-316.

Severin, F.T. ed. *Humanistic Viewpoints in Psychology.* New York: McGraw-Hill, 1965.

-----. *Discovering Man in Psychology--A Humanistic Approach.* New York: McGraw-Hill, 1973.

Seeman, M., and Evans, J.M. "Alienation and Learning in a Hospital Setting." *American Sociological Review,* 1962, 27, pp. 772-83.

Shapiro, A.K. "A Historic and Heuristic Definition of the Placebo." *Psychiatry,* 1964, 27, pp. 52-58.

Sherif, M., and Cantril, H. *The Psychology of Ego-Involvements*. New York: Wiley, 1947.

Shorkey, C.T., and Reyes, E. "Relationship Between Self-Actualization and Rational Thinking." *Psychological Reports*, 1978, 42, p. 842.

Shostrom, E. *Personal Orientation Inventory (POI): A Test of Self-Actualization*. San Diego, Calif., Educational and Industrial Testing Service, 1963.

-----. "An Inventory for Measurement of Self-Actualization." *Educational and Psychological Measurement*, 1964, 24, pp. 207-18.

Slepova, T.V. "A Critical Analysis from the Problem of Self-Acutalization in Some Investigation of Humanistic Psychology." *Voprosy Psykhologii*, 1976, 5, pp. 163-70.

Smith, B. "On Self-Acutalization: A Trans-Ambivalent Examination of Focal Theme in Maslow's Psychology." *Journal of Humanistic Psychology*, 1973, 13, pp. 18-33.

Smith, H. *Forgotten Truth: The Primordial Tradition*. New York: Harper and Row, 1976.

Smith, M.B. "Perspectives on Selfhood." *American Psychologist*, 1978, 33, pp. 1053-63.

-----. "Psychology and Humanism." *Journal of Humanistic Psychology*, 1982, 22, pp. 44-55.

Smithers, A.G., and Lobley, D.M. "Dogmatism, Social Attitudes and Personality." *British Journal of Social and Clinical Psychology*, 1978, 17, pp. 135-42.

Snygg, D., and Combs, A.W. *Individual Behaviour*. New York: Harper and Row, 1949.

Strickland, B.R, and Crowne, D.P. "Conformity under Conditions of Simulated Group Pressure as a Function of the Need for Social Approval." *Journal of Social Psychology*, 1962, 58, pp. 171-81.

Sussy, C. "A Study of the Adequacy of Abraham Maslow's Concept of the Self to the Theory of Self-Acutalization." *Dissertation Abstracts International*, 1978, 38, 5548-49.

Sutich, A. *American Association for Humanistic Psychology: Progress Report*. Palo Alto, California, November, 1962.

Sward, K. "Self-Actualization and Women: Rank and Freud Contrasted." *Journal of Humanistic Psychology*, 1980, 20.

Thomas, H.F. "Self-Actualization through the Group Experience." *Journal of Humanistic Psychology*, 1968, pp. 39-44.

Thorndike, E.L. *Personal Selection-Tests and Measurement Techniques*. New York: Wiley, 1949.

Treppa, J.A., and Fricke, L. "Effects of a Marathon Group Experience." *Journal of Consulting Psychology*, 1972, 19, pp. 466-67.

Unger, S.N. "Masculine, L.S.D. Psilocybin and Personality Change." In Solomon, D., ed., *L.S.D. The Consciousness-Expanding*. New York: Putnam, 1964.

Whitaker, C.A., and Warkentin, J. "The Therapist as a Prototype." In J.F.T. Bugental, ed., *Challenges of Humanistic Psychology*.

Wilkins, W.E. and Krause, H. "Anxiety and Actualization: Further Research." *Journal of Clinical Psychology*, 1978, 34, pp. 958-60.

Williams, J.E. "Acceptance by Others and Its Relationship to Acceptance of Self and Others: A Report of Fey's Study." *Journal of Abnormal and Social Psychology*, 1962, 65, pp. 438-42.

William, B., and Arndt, Jr. *Theories of Personality*. New York: Macmillan, 1974.

Wilson, C. "Existential Psychology: A Novelist's Approach." In J.F.T. Bugental, ed., *Challenges of Humanistic Psychology*.

Wuthnow, R. "Peak Experience: Some Empirical Tests." *Journal of Humanistic Psychology*, 1983, 3.

Zigler, E., and Phillips, L. "Social-Competence: The Action Thought Parameter and Vicariousness in Normal and Pathological Behaviors." *Journal of Abnormal and Social Psychology*, 1961, 63, pp. 137-46.

Zuckerman, M., Baer, M., and Monashkin, I. "Acceptance of Self, Parents and People in Patients and Normals." *Journal of Clinical Psychology*, 1956, 12, pp. 327-32.

Index